M000190971

INVESTING FOR BEGINNERS

Quick-Start Guide

INVESTING
for BEGINNERS

ESSENTIALS TO START INVESTING WISELY

TYCHO
PRESS

Copyright © 2014 by Tycho Press, Berkeley, California

No part of this publication may be reproduced, stored in a retrieval system or transmitted in any form or by any means, electronic, mechanical, photocopying, recording, scanning or otherwise, except as permitted under Section 107 or 108 of the 1976 United States Copyright Act, without the prior written permission of the publisher. Requests to the publisher for permission should be addressed to the Permissions Department, Tycho Press, 918 Parker St., Suite A-12, Berkeley, CA 94710.

Limit of Liability/Disclaimer of Warranty The publisher and the author make no representations or warranties with respect to the accuracy or completeness of the contents of this work and specifically disclaim all warranties, including without limitation warranties of fitness for a particular purpose. No warranty may be created or extended by sales or promotional materials. The advice and strategies contained herein may not be suitable for every situation. This work is sold with the understanding that the publisher is not engaged in rendering medical, legal or other professional advice or services. If professional assistance is required, the services of a competent professional person should be sought. Neither the publisher nor the author shall be liable for damages arising herefrom. The fact that an individual, organization, or website is referred to in this work as a citation and/or potential source of further information does not mean that the author or the publisher endorses the information the individual, organization or website may provide or recommendations they/it may make. Further, readers should be aware that Internet websites listed in this work may have changed or disappeared between when this work was written and when it is read.

For general information on our other products and services or to obtain technical support, please contact our Customer Care Department within the United States at (866) 744-2665, or outside the United States at (510) 253-0500.

Tycho Press publishes its books in a variety of electronic and print formats. Some content that appears in print may not be available in electronic books, and vice versa.

TRADEMARKS Tycho Press and the Tycho Press logo are trademarks or registered trademarks of Callisto Media Inc. and/or its affiliates, in the United States and other countries, and may not be used without written permission. All other trademarks are the property of their respective owners. Tycho Press is not associated with any product or vendor mentioned in this book.

ISBN Softcover 978-1-62315-445-5 | eBook 978-1-62315-446-2

Contents

An investment in knowledge always pays the best interest.

BENJAMIN FRANKLIN
THE WAY TO WEALTH: BEN FRANKLIN ON MONEY AND SUCCESS

Understanding Investments

If you haven't yet begun to invest, it's time to get started. If you already invest, you should probably step it up. If you already have more than enough set aside, realize that the word *enough* is at best a shoddy estimate, at worst a pipe dream.

Like so many of life's most important tasks, investing is simple at its core. You deploy money in the hopes of receiving more back than you put in. Like paying for college to open up a career path or buying that Ken Griffey, Jr., rookie card on eBay, you deploy money in the hopes of getting back more than you originally invest.

We all understand the concept of investing. Unfortunately, way too many of us make the process more complicated than necessary.

Admittedly, some investments require sophistication and a deep knowledge of finance. Unless you've studied the markets and understand how they work, don't let a slick talker persuade you to invest in credit default swaps, option straddles, or venture capital. All three of those investments can generate profits, and all make sense for investors in certain situations. But if you can't explain the investment to someone who isn't an expert, you have no business making it. By the time you finish this book, you'll be ready to clear that explanatory hurdle with most of the investments you encounter.

Part of understanding investments involves knowing how they work and what you can accomplish by using them. However, knowledge of investments will not make you a successful investor on its own. You must also understand the markets themselves, what moves them, and which moves warrant attention.

But even if you master knowledge of investments and markets, you won't make it far without another type of knowledge: an understanding of yourself, your strengths and weaknesses, and your needs and capabilities.

Investor after investor has leaped into the financial pool ill equipped for the swim. You've probably met one of them: the guy who complains that Wall Street is rigged, or that he never gets a break, or that everyone else is lucky except him. Most of you probably know several of these tortured souls, battered and discouraged not because investing has been too tough for them but simply because they haven't prepared well enough.

Never before has information been easier to obtain. At the click of a mouse, you can find not only the price of an investment but also fundamental data underpinning that price, news about the company, and in some cases the opinions of professional analysts who track the security. So separate yourself from the pack not only by acquiring information, but by learning how to use it.

PART I

Investing
Basics

THE MORE YOU KNOW, THE BETTER YOUR DECISIONS

Never forget that the purpose of investing is to make money. That concept sounds simplistic, but many investors get caught up in the spectacle and forget the goal of the exercise. You don't invest to impress your friends, or to make interesting dinner conversation, or to feel better about yourself. After all, didn't you come to this shindig with the intention of leaving wealthier than when you arrived?

The key to making money in the market isn't mastering esoteric financial concepts or getting in on the hot, new investment. It just takes learning the basics, keeping it simple, and not making stupid mistakes. Legendary investor Warren Buffett probably put it best when he said: "You only have to do a very few things right in your life so long as you don't do too many things wrong."

Buffett may be the second-wealthiest man in the United States, but he makes a point of keeping things simple. Famous for his reluctance to invest in anything he doesn't understand, Buffett gauges the appeal of his investments in part by how effectively he thinks he could explain their benefits to his sisters, two intelligent women who don't know much about finance.

Will this book turn you into the Oracle of Omaha overnight? No. But it can help you make better sense of the investment landscape. Its logic is the more you know, the better decisions you can make. If, after learning more about investments, you will realize that if you still can't see an "investment opportunity," step away and let someone else take the chance on it.

Don't let the opinions of the average man sway you. Dream, and he thinks you're crazy. Succeed, and he thinks you're lucky. Acquire wealth, and he thinks you're greedy. Pay no attention. He simply doesn't understand.

ROBERT GRAY ALLEN
BUSINESSMAN AND MEMBER OF THE U.S. HOUSE OF REPRESENTATIVES

1

DEFINE YOUR GOALS

Most people understand the need to invest. After all, they will retire someday and need to fund their lifestyle without drawing on earnings from a job. That reality drives tens of millions to place their money into a stock or commodity that they think will produce returns. But not all investors—or investment strategies—are created equal.

Way too many people start investing without a plan. Driven by a vague knowledge that they need to build wealth for the future, they read a stock tip in an online newsletter or take advice from a brother-in-law who says a stock "will go through the roof."

The problem is that even if the newsletter editor or brother-in-law provides good advice on which stock to pick, that investment may not fit you or your goals. Unfortunately, you won't be able to tell the good investments from the bad unless you *know* your goals. That means writing them down, not keeping them locked in your head.

The Planning for the Future worksheet on page 18 will help you identify your goals. Once you've noted those goals, save them and use them for future reference.

Five Steps Toward Setting the Right Goals

1. **Be honest.** Don't write down a goal just because your parents or friends have achieved it. For example, if your uncle retired at 50 and loved it, don't necessarily assume you want to do the same. Early retirement won't work for everyone. Some people don't have the personality to adapt to such a slowdown. Think about how you want to spend your future; then identify goals that fit that vision. Don't be

afraid to think big. A person who achieves every one of her goals probably didn't aim high enough.

2. **Don't rush.** When you fill out your worksheet, be sure to use a pencil, because you may need to make some edits. Even when you're looking at goals for 25 years in the future, take into consideration that your outlook can differ from month to month, or even day to day. So after you record your goals, return to the list in a week, and then again in a couple more weeks. Don't consider the goals official until you've allowed them to marinate for a while.

3. **Consider timing.** An 18-year-old reading this book may have a five-year goal of completing college with less than $10,000 in student loan debt. A 38-year-old with $100,000 in retirement assets might have a target of achieving a $150,000 portfolio in five years. A 58-year-old's five-year goal may revolve around acquiring property in the community where she intends to retire. Your goals are just that—uniquely yours. Your age, career status, and financial position will affect those goals.

4. **Don't lock yourself in.** Over time, your goals will change. This doesn't mean you will backtrack; it just means that life doesn't travel in a simple linear path. Goals you set early in life, when you earn $12 per hour and eat peanut-butter-and-jelly sandwiches for three meals a day, probably won't apply 15 years later. When you're married, with two kids and a third on the way, living in a $200,000 house and earning $75,000 per year, the goal of saving $50 a month won't mean as much as it did during the leaner years. While you should never change your goals just for the sake of change, you will want to refine them as your needs change.

5. **Keep your goals close.** Goals written on a sheet of paper and shoved into the back of a dark closet won't help you. Unless you refer to your goals at least once a year (every six months is even better), they'll add about as much value to your life as the dusty treadmill you never use.

Know Your Investment Personality

The lure of investments appeals to all kinds of people. It is important to start by determining your investment personality. The sooner you know where you fit, the better you can plan your financial future. Most people fall into one of three categories: thrill seekers, worriers, or plodders.

Thrill Seekers

Thrill seekers are the guys who jump into the front seat on the roller coaster every time. This type of investor takes on a lot of risk and will plant his feet and laugh at a storm while everyone else heads indoors.

THREE TIPS FOR THRILL SEEKERS

1. **Don't waste time trying to change your nature.** Acknowledge who you are and plan accordingly. Thrill seekers who try to quit cold turkey often jump back into risky behavior without warning. And sudden change rarely makes investment sense.

2. **Talk to the experts.** No matter how much you welcome risk, you can't afford to let those personal desires torpedo your long-term financial happiness. The problem with a double-or-nothing attitude is that one mistake can erode the product of dozens— even hundreds—of past successes. Avoid that temptation by allowing someone else to manage your money or closely following the recommendations of a third party. Find a financial adviser or newsletter that relies on a system you understand and appreciate. Then do what they say, when they say it, allowing an impartial stranger to offset your tendency to dive into the pool without checking for water.

3. **Keep some mad money.** While where you place the bulk of your funds should be determined by a disciplined investment system, you can maintain sanity and blow off steam by indulging your passions—a little bit. Consider slipping $5 of every $100 you invest into a separate brokerage account that you manage yourself. Take the risks you want with that money. If they pay off, great; if not, you haven't lost anything you needed. Set a cap on your mad-money account. Whenever the account rises above that cap, pull out the excess cash and stash it in your primary account. If you run out of mad money, replenish the account slowly as you beef up the primary account.

Worriers

The opposite of the thrill seeker, the worrier focuses on the negative—on what she might lose more than the possibility for gain. Now, some caution and skepticism is healthy. Remember the risks the thrill seeker embraces? Most people wisely take on somewhat less risk. But worriers can take risk management too far.

Worriers often choose to save rather than invest, stashing most of their money in savings accounts, certificates of deposit, and other cash vehicles. In a vacuum, saving isn't bad. It certainly helps wealth building more than spending does. However, over time, savings accounts and other no-risk investments are pretty much guaranteed to underperform riskier types of investments. In fact, most savings vehicles will deliver a return that is less than the rate of inflation, so the purchasing power of a portfolio can actually decline over time.

Bottom line: Worriers tend to load up on low-risk, low-return investments. Although they're less likely to suffer large losses, they're more likely to earn subpar returns. Investors face many types of risk. Worriers focus on the potential for volatility (a

THREE TIPS FOR WORRIERS

1. **Don't fear your own conservatism.** An innate dislike of risk can benefit you in many facets of life. If you're a worrier, you probably drive more carefully, plan vacations in great detail, and rarely get caught in the rain without an umbrella. If that approach makes you happy, more power to you. Just be aware of the risks of an overly conservative approach to investing.

2. **Keep your eye off the money.** Yes, this sounds like the opposite of what the financial experts say. In this context, the advice pertains simply to not following the performance of your investments too closely from day to day. By all means, pay attention to what investments you own and make changes when needed. However, you'll be happier and your portfolio will be better off if you don't check the Internet every day to see how your stocks are doing. Stocks rise and fall constantly, and if you know you can't handle the volatility, stop checking prices all the time. Unless you find a company-specific problem, limit yourself to checking on the portfolio's prices once a week.

3. **Focus on passive investment options.** (You'll read more about passive versus active investments in chapter 5). Passive investments allow you to not put a lot of time into determining whether XYZ Widgets looks better than ABC Gizmos. These types of investments, which include index funds, simply track segments of the market. Such investments limit your exposure to the risks that come with reliance on an individual company.

wide variance in returns from period to period) and the risk of loss (the chance that an investment loses money). By overcompensating for the risk of losses with low-risk investments, investors face the possibility that their investment portfolio might not meet their financial goals, which could force them to downsize their lifestyle or retire later than they hoped.

Plodders

The third type of investor has the trait that makes it easiest to succeed in the investment world: patience.

Investors might read books like this one, as well as newspapers and newsletters, to learn more about investing and about individual companies. They may create spreadsheets to compare data on different investments and research securities getting right down to what a company's CEO eats for breakfast. Both strategies will help you succeed. But an investor's biggest, most powerful ally isn't knowledge—it's time.

The more time you have to invest, the more opportunities you'll have to add funds to your portfolio, and the more you can afford to ride out weakness. If you believe

---

THREE TIPS FOR PLODDERS

1. **Keep the faith.** The word *plodder* connotes slow movement, and often a simplistic approach. When markets are booming, thrill seekers will dismiss you as outmoded. When markets plummet, worriers will question why you're still following the same course. But the financial world rewards consistency.

2. **Do your research up-front.** Plodders succeed because they find a system that works, then stick with it through the good times and the bad. This strategy assumes you've identified a truly superior system. But the very consistency that wins battles can lose them just as easily if you consistently make bad choices. Settle on a system that works, and then stick with it.

3. **Don't fear change.** Yes, on the surface this sounds like a contradiction to the very nature of being a plodder. Too many people refuse to revise their thinking for any reason. But markets change, as will your financial condition and investment objectives. When the reason for an investment decision no longer applies, wise investors regroup and make a different decision. Don't get caught in today's market using yesterday's tactics.

---

the stock market will rise at an 8 percent annual rate over the next 20 years and you don't plan on touching your money until those 20 years end, then you need not panic if the market declines 10 percent in your first year of investing. The portfolio will have 19 years to grow after the decline, presumably benefiting from the securities you purchased when prices were low. If you're starting later in life and don't have 40, 20, or even 10 years to build wealth, you can still plod toward a richer future. Investing doesn't work miracles, but plodders never expect miracles anyway.

Bottom line: Plodders have built-in advantages over thrill seekers and worriers when it comes to investing. They can avoid the low-percentage moves that lead thrill seekers astray, and they're willing to sample a broader variety of investment options than worriers. Does this mean that plodders are guaranteed success? No more than thrill seekers and worriers are guaranteed failure. Plodders can make mistakes just like everyone else. The purpose of this book is to help you minimize those mistakes.

Five Types of Investor

By now, you've probably determined what type of investment personality you have. Of course, many kinds of people fall within these groupings, which means you can't select an investment approach based solely on the broad characteristics outlined.

The next few pages will help you dig deeper into your investment personality. Many investment approaches can allow you to make money, as long as you understand their strengths and weaknesses. The following pages break investors down into five types that should encompass every reader of this book. If you identify with more than one of the types, don't panic; many people fit into multiple categories.

TYPE 1 ▶ *Data Crunchers*

If you're old enough to read this book, you probably already know whether you have the skills, desire, and temperament to do your own investment research. The task isn't for everyone, but most data crunchers won't be happy letting someone else tell them how to invest.

While the ability to interpret data represents a competitive advantage in the investing game, it can also weigh you down. Investment statistics come in all types and in exhaustive detail. An investor could spend weeks researching a single stock, drilling down into the guts of the company at a level of detail forensic accountants fear. At some point, you must consider the research completed and make a decision.

Many data crunchers suffer from paralysis by analysis, overloading themselves with so much information that they have trouble making decisions. To combat this, either decide in advance what information you wish to compile and review or set yourself a hard deadline to finish your analysis. At that point, interpret and act.

Bottom line: While numbers never tell the whole story—and paralysis by analysis is a genuine risk—data crunchers always have an edge. Although there are a variety of personalities and approaches, if you intend to make your own investment decisions, you'd better be comfortable with numbers. If you aren't statistics savvy, don't fear; plenty of successful investors don't spend much time looking at financial statements. Instead, they rely on the wisdom and analysis of others.

TYPE 2 ▶ *Headliners*

When you invest in an individual stock or bond, you are purchasing a piece of a company. Any time you commit to such an investment, you also sign up to follow the company's news. Investors of all stripes, even those who take the advice of others, should read the financial press and follow stories about financial markets and the forces that move them. Knowledge truly is power. Pay attention to headlines pertaining to a company in which you've invested. If you own stock in XYZ Widgets but don't read the company's latest declaration of quarterly profits, you have no excuse when the stock blindsides you. Knowledgeable investors make better decisions.

Now, just because you follow the news doesn't make you a headliner. Headliners make, buy, and sell decisions based mostly on what they read. Such a strategy usually leads down a bad path. You see, financial markets are a giant discounting engine that values securities based on the present value of future cash flows. Markets take into account current conditions and what conditions the investment world's decision makers expect in the future, then distill that news into today's prices. If economists expect the labor market to slow, those expectations will manifest in prices for securities.

Investors make money in individual stocks and bonds by identifying the ones that are mispriced by the market. When you see that economists' forecast for annual gross domestic product have risen and decide to buy stocks sensitive to the economy in response, you're too late. The smart money has already made those buys, if in fact the buys made sense in the first place. By the time the average investor reads about an economic trend in the *Wall Street Journal*, professional investors have already acted on the news.

This lack of evenness in news distribution irritates individual investors, but don't fall into the trap of writing it off as unfair. The professionals on Wall Street are paid to keep up with economic developments and sector-related trends, while the average investor is busy with other responsibilities most of the time. Those who invest part time start out with a disadvantage relative to those who invest for a living. Does this mean the small investor can't make money? Not at all. However, the small investor will have a lot of trouble trying to profit from news on economic or political activity that affects stocks.

Of course, if you encounter company-specific news, the picture changes. Once again, you can't expect to act as fast as the professionals. But headlines that pertain to a specific company are more likely to directly affect that company's stocks or bonds than would a broader piece of economic news. So take the time to keep up with the news about companies you own stock in.

Bottom line: When you hear something bad (or good) about a company, it's natural to want to sell (or buy) on that news. But the best investors don't overreact to headlines. Investments often decline in value on bad news, then bounce back, regaining some or all of the lost ground as the market self-corrects. Even with company-specific news, you should never assume you've figured out what everyone else is missing, or that a security will react as you suspect. Veteran investors can tell you of countless times when a company declared earnings that fell short of expectations, yet the shares rose because of other information. In general, headlines are a poor driver of investment decisions.

TYPE 3 ▶ *Tip Seekers*

Has anyone ever offered you a stock tip? "This company can't lose." "I know the CEO, and she's buying stock in bunches." And perhaps the most insidious: "Didn't you hear about Presto Drug's new treatment for arthritis? The new drug generated more than $100 million in sales last quarter."

Yes, the company *can* lose, even if your neighbor swears by it. Sometimes CEOs buy stock at the wrong time, and sometimes a tipster will lie, claiming a relationship with the CEO when all he did was sit in the same section with her at a baseball game.

The last type of tip, one based on positive factual information, can be the toughest to resist. Who wouldn't want to buy stock in a company making a dynamite new drug? The problem with such tips dovetails with the reason why investing based on headlines often fails to pay off. Everybody following that stock knows about the drug. Yes, it's selling well. But in most cases, the market has already baked those sales into the stock's price.

In addition, no matter how well a company performs or how fast a stock helps increase its sales or profits, you don't want to pay too much. No matter how good the investment, no matter how strong the company, the price can rise high enough so the purchase no longer makes sense.

Bottom line: Sometimes tipsters give you good advice. But when you buy on a tip, you don't have all the information concerning the purchase, so you don't know for sure whether you've paid a good price. If you can't demonstrate a solid reason for buying, how will you know when to sell? You won't.

TYPE 4 ▸ *System Users*

On Wall Street, you may hear the adage "Everybody's got a system." However, that statement doesn't hold water. Millions of people invest without a system, which is tantamount to setting off on a cross-country bike race without a map. Systems come in all shapes, most revolving around a few core investment methods:

- **Quantitative analysis.** The systems depending on this type of analysis gauge stocks based on a variety of data, such as sales, profits, cash flows, debt levels, profitability measurements, valuation ratios, and price action. Quantitative analysts build statistical models to identify stocks that look good based on a large number of data points.
- **Qualitative analysis.** Systems that use this type of analysis consider nonquantifiable information, such as new-product pipelines, research prowess, quality of management, and industry trends.
- **Technical analysis.** The systems involved here interpret chart patterns and other trading data. Investors analyze a security's past performance and draw conclusions about its likely future path.
- **Momentum.** These systems zero in on stocks that have performed very well in recent trading, hoping to catch the wave before it crests.

FIVE WAYS TO IDENTIFY A BAD INVESTMENT SYSTEM

The financial markets abound with investment systems. What follows are some danger signs to look out for. If the system you're considering has any of these characteristics, move on. You can do better.

1. **Unexplainable.** Some investment advisers develop complicated systems. Given the complexity of financial markets, you shouldn't dismiss such systems out of hand. However, if the adviser can't explain the system to your satisfaction, the problem lies with the adviser or her system, not with you. If she can't break her system down into chunks a lay investor can understand, then she doesn't know the system well enough for you to trust it.

2. **Untrackable.** Just about every investment system provides data on returns you can follow and compare to that of other systems as well as to that of the broader market. If your adviser won't provide you with this data—preferably for a number of years—then you have the wrong adviser. Those returns should reflect the entire list of recommended stocks, not just a sample. Any adviser can look good if she only tells you about her winners.

3. **Inappropriate.** Regardless of the quality of the system or how much you trust the adviser who developed it, don't invest if the securities are a bad fit. A conservative investor shouldn't sink most of her money into a system that revolves around small company stocks or risky derivatives. Consider both the system's potential returns and its risk before making a decision.

4. **Unbelievable.** Nobody has ever come up with an investment system that wins every time. Unfortunately, plenty of advisers claim they've done it. Those people are lying about their performance, which means you can't trust anything else they say.

5. **Expensive.** When you review historical returns, consider them with fees taken out. After all, if you invest, you'll pay those fees. If the adviser evades questions about fees, either current or historical, look elsewhere for investment advice.

These aren't the only methods, just the best known. Investors can make money using any or all of them, but some methods work better than others.

While data crunchers tend to develop their own systems based on the types of statistics they analyze, other types of investors glom onto a system developed by someone else. Such investors provide most of the support for the financial-newsletter industry.

Investors who rely on a system generally receive regular advice regarding what to buy and sell. Most of the best purveyors of financial advice will track the specific portfolios that contain their recommendations.

Bottom line: Systems of analysis benefit investors in two chief ways: First, they allow individuals to tap into the research of experts. Second, they offer a level of discipline, providing buying and selling advice from people presumably less likely to become emotionally attached to their investments. On the downside, to some extent you've put your future in the hands of a third party. Such an action makes sense for millions of investors, but some don't want to delegate any responsibility. Regardless of the type of system you choose to use, make sure you understand how it works. There is more than one way to make money in the market, and you should settle on one that makes you feel comfortable. If your investments keep you up at night, you're holding the wrong investments.

TYPE 5 ▶ *Outsourcers*

Outsourcers are investors who entrust their portfolio management to a professional who does the buying and selling. The preceding advice regarding investment systems applies to this approach as well, with a few caveats.

Most investment systems worth using will cost a few bucks. While you can subscribe to any number of quality newsletters for $300 per year or less, professional money managers usually charge fees based on the size of the account. For traditional management of portfolios containing stocks and mutual funds, you can expect to pay in the neighborhood of 1.25 percent, often with sliding scales for larger accounts.

Some money managers use nonstandard systems, such as performance fees that change based on how the portfolio performs relative to a benchmark. Alternately, they could roll everything into a wrap fee—a flat fee that includes management expenses, commissions, and any other administrative charges. Before you invest, make sure you understand the manager's fee structure.

In some cases, the manager will pass on the trading costs assessed by the broker that holds the account. Such managers don't profit from your trades. If the manager charges her own trading fee, take a look at the firm's trading activity. When a manager makes a profit every time she trades, she has an incentive to trade, possibly more often than she should. These advisers receive commissions from fund companies or other investment firms in exchange for purchasing certain securities for client portfolios. You want an adviser who has nothing to gain by putting you in specific securities, and instead will seek to keep your business by providing you with the best possible investment performance.

Before signing up with a money-management firm, make sure you understand its system and trust the person who handles your portfolio. Reputable firms will provide you with references if you request them. Call the names they give you and ask the clients about the quality of service, how closely the manager hewed to promised strategy, and the account's performance. When you check references, keep in mind that the manager will provide you only the names of clients she knows will speak well of her.

Bottom line: Not all investment managers are created equal. Choose carefully, and ensure that the manager sticks with an investment style you understand and appreciate. Going with a professional manager doesn't make you lazy or uncaring. Some people care about personal finance but just don't have much interest in managing an investment portfolio. For others, the decision boils down to time. It takes several hours a week to effectively manage a diversified portfolio. If you can't devote enough time to do the job right, don't hesitate to hire someone to handle the task for you, in the same way that you wouldn't balk at taking your car to a mechanic or seeing a lawyer if someone sues you.

When it comes to investing, there are hundreds of ways to skin the cat. Find one that resonates with you; then pursue it with discipline.

WORKSHEET 1.1 PLANNING FOR THE FUTURE

This worksheet features three sections to accommodate your goals for the near term (next 5 years), moderate term (next 15 years), and long term (25 years or more). Of course, those labels are relative, depending on your age. Just remember that this is your goal sheet, not a school paper that you must share with other people. Based on your age and your progress on the financial journey, set goals that make sense for you and your family. Understand that your goals will change over time, especially those for periods farther out.

Whenever possible, tie a dollar amount to the goal. Of course, some goals—for instance, retiring early—may not lend themselves to a specific funding target.

SHORT-TERM GOALS

Personal _____

Professional _____

Charitable_____

Other_____

MODERATE-TERM GOALS

Personal _____

Professional _____

Charitable_____

Other_____

LONG-TERM GOALS

Personal _____

Professional _____

Charitable_____

Other_____

SIGNS OF SUCCESS

Success is one of those words not easily explained by a dictionary. The problem with measuring success lies in determining the proper scale. How much wealth is enough? Ask 100 people and you might receive 100 different answers.

Instead of trying to define success in specific financial terms, focus on achieving a goal. With that in mind, list three things you must accomplish to consider your investing a success. Possible signs of success include owning a paid-off home by age 55, operating a successful business, or saving $300 per month, adjusted for inflation over time.

1. _____

2. _____

3. _____

Most people fail to realize that in life, it's not how much money you make, it's how much money you keep.

ROBERT KIYOSAKI
RICH DAD, POOR DAD

2

HOW MUCH WILL YOU NEED?

So it's time to set a target. You know the type of investor you are. Now you must blend that with your long-term goals and come up with some hard numbers. If you haven't already completed the Planning for the Future worksheet on page 18, do it now. You'll get more benefit out of the next few pages if you have a firm idea of what you hope to accomplish. Only you can determine how much you'll need. To begin, check out the cost calculators in the following box.

While college, home ownership, and retirement represent the three largest expenses most people will encounter, they aren't the only ones. Consider the goals laid out on your worksheet, then calculate how much you'll need to meet them. While the calculations can be tedious, anybody who passed a high school math class can handle them.

For example, Joe Investor wants to quit his job in 10 years and purchase a fast-food franchise for $200,000. He has $50,000 saved. How much does he need to invest to meet his goal? This question involves only four numbers, two of which you already know:

- *Initial investment*: $50,000
- *Time horizon*: 10 years
- *Likely investment returns*: ??
- *Annual investment*: ??

Once he has any three of those numbers, Joe can calculate the fourth. To start out, Joe estimates that he can spare $15,000 per year to invest for the franchise and that he will earn 8 percent on his investments. Based on those numbers, Joe comes up with a spreadsheet (see Table 2.1).

TABLE 2.1 WHAT YOU NEED TO GET WHERE YOU'RE GOING		
EXAMPLE #1		
Annual contribution	$15,000	
Expected returns	8%	
	Investment	**Portfolio Value**
Current assets	$50,000	$50,000
Year 1	$15,000	$69,000
Year 2	$15,000	$89,520
Year 3	$15,000	$111,682
Year 4	$15,000	$135,616
Year 5	$15,000	$161,465
Year 6	$15,000	$189,383
Year 7	$15,000	$219,533
Year 8	$15,000	$252,096
Year 9	$15,000	$287,264
Year 10	$15,000	$325,245

To see how Joe came up with his numbers—and to learn how to do the calculations for yourself—set up your own Excel spreadsheet and follow these steps:

1. Create row and column headers like those in Table 2.1.
2. Next to Annual Contribution, type in $15,000.
3. Next to Expected Returns, type in 8%.
4. In the Investment column for Year 1, type in an equal sign and the number of the cell containing the annual contribution. Doing so will move the value from the original cell to the one with the equal sign.
5. For the future-year contributions in the Investment column, again type an equal sign and the cell number.
6. In the Portfolio Value column for Year 1, multiply the portfolio value from the cell above it ($50,000) by 1.08 (1 + annual return), to get $54,000. Add the investment listed in the column, $15,000, to come up with a total of $69,000.
7. For the Portfolio Value for Year 2, use the same equation, linking the result to the cell immediately above. The Portfolio Value reaches $89,520. The calculation works the same way as the previous one but starts with the $69,000 Joe had at the end of Year 1 instead of his $50,000 initial investment.

TABLE 2.2 WHAT YOU NEED TO GET WHERE YOU'RE GOING		
EXAMPLE #2		
Annual contribution	$10,000	
Expected returns	8%	
Target	$250,000	
	Investment	**Portfolio Value**
Current assets	$50,000	$50,000
Year 1	$10,000	$64,000
Year 2	$10,000	$79,120
Year 3	$10,000	$95,450
Year 4	$10,000	$113,086
Year 5	$10,000	$132,132
Year 6	$10,000	$152,703
Year 7	$10,000	$174,919
Year 8	$10,000	$198,913
Year 9	$10,000	$224,826
Year 10	$10,000	$252,812

Following those steps, you'll find that if Joe invests $15,000 per year, earning 8 percent returns on his money, he'll have $325,245 at the end of 10 years. Joe doesn't mind overbudgeting, because he might not earn the expected 8 percent and the situation could change, leaving him with less than $15,000 available to invest. Still, $325,245 exceeds his $200,000 goal by more than 62 percent, and he doesn't want to overbudget *that* much. Instead, he decides to target $250,000, figuring that if he shoots for a target 25 percent above the actual amount needed, he'll leave enough wiggle room to cope with the unexpected.

Joe adds a row to his spreadsheet to accommodate the $250,000 target. Then to get to $250,000 at the end of Year 10, he plays around with his assumptions, reducing the amount he invests to $10,000 a year instead of the $15,000 he planned initially. Joe revises his spreadsheet (see Table 2.2).

Joe likes the numbers he comes up with better than those from his first effort. However, he worries that he might not be able to earn an 8 percent investment return consistently. So he tries again, keeping the annual investment at $15,000 but lowering the target investment return to 4 percent (see Table 2.3).

TABLE 2.3 WHAT YOU NEED TO GET WHERE YOU'RE GOING		
EXAMPLE #3		
Annual contribution	$15,000	
Expected returns	4%	
Target	$250,000	
	Investment	**Portfolio Value**
Current assets	$50,000	$50,000
Year 1	$15,000	$67,000
Year 2	$15,000	$84,680
Year 3	$15,000	$103,067
Year 4	$15,000	$122,190
Year 5	$15,000	$142,077
Year 6	$15,000	$162,761
Year 7	$15,000	$184,271
Year 8	$15,000	$206,642
Year 9	$15,000	$229,908
Year 10	$15,000	$254,104

Of course, the numbers and goals you came up with probably don't match Joe's. But you just created a powerful tool to build your own financial models that are right for your own situation. If you need more years, add the rows. If instead you wish to calculate an investment with a five-year time horizon, then stop at Year 5. Remember, all you need to create this model is four numbers: the initial investment, annual contribution, expected investment return, and a target portfolio value. Using a spreadsheet you develop yourself, you can adjust all of the assumptions.

The goals you wrote down on your worksheet should provide a solid starting place. If you don't know exactly how much you'll need for expenses in the future, just give it your best estimate. By now, you've already seen some of the tools for dealing with questionable estimates, and the coming pages will offer more examples.

Three Plans for Three Purposes

Joe finished his financial work and was last seen flipping burgers in his new restaurant. But you have just gotten started. To demonstrate the versatility of your Excel model, work up some targets for other financial goals. Start with the "Big 3": college, home, and retirement goals. As a model, follow the story of Nancy Nickel, who has saved up a lot of money, but until now hasn't done much planning with it.

CALCULATING COSTS: WHERE TO BEGIN?

- Saving for college? Visit CNNMoney's college cost calculator for a cost estimate (Cgi.money.cnn.com/tools/collegecost/collegecost.html).

- Saving for a home? Visit Bankrate's mortgage calculator to compute your payment (Bankrate.com/calculators/mortgages/mortgage-calculator.aspx).

- Saving for retirement? CNNMoney's retirement calculator can help you determine how much you'll need (Money.cnn.com/calculator/retirement/retirement-need/).

PLAN 1 ▶ *Saving for College*

Nancy's daughter Nikki just turned seven. Nikki will start college in 12 years, and her mother hopes she will attend her own alma mater, the University of Southern California. From CNNMoney's college cost calculator, Nancy learns that tuition, fees, room and board, and books cost just over $63,000 per year. She can expect to pay $152,500 for her daughter's tuition for four years, taking into account the average amount of grants and scholarships received by families in her income bracket.

So Nancy should set a target of $152,500, right? Not at all. She must take into account two financial forces nobody can escape: inflation and the risk of bad estimates.

First, this cost estimate assumes Nikki will attend school at the current tuition rates. However, in 12 years, costs will have risen. According to the College Savings Plans Network, tuition inflation has averaged 6–7 percent annually for many years. Taking this into consideration, Nancy adjusts $152,500 for a 7 percent annual inflation rate for 12 years, yielding a target of nearly $345,000.

Second, Nancy wants to engineer the financial plans in excess of the estimated amount, in case her investment returns end up falling short of what she predicted. For example, investors who plan as if they will earn 10 percent, then actually earn 8 percent, may fail to meet their goals. So Nancy overbudgets college costs by 20 percent and sets a target of $415,000.

Nancy has already saved $100,000 and can afford to invest up to $12,000 per year. Annual returns of 6.5 percent would meet the goal achieved at that rate of investment. However, Nancy believes she can do better with her investments. Assuming she would be able to earn a 10 percent return, Nancy figures she could invest just $5,000 per year and end up with enough to pay for college. She settles on a middle ground, deciding that 8 percent returns is realistic, which means $9,000 a year in additional investment would do the job (see Table 2.4).

TABLE 2.4 SAVING FOR COLLEGE		
Annual contribution	$9,000	
Expected returns	8%	
Target	$415,000	
	Investment	Portfolio Value
Current assets	$50,000	$100,000
Year 1	$9,000	$117,000
Year 2	$9,000	$135,360
Year 3	$9,000	$155,189
Year 4	$9,000	$176,604
Year 5	$9,000	$199,732
Year 6	$9,000	$224,711
Year 7	$9,000	$251,688
Year 8	$9,000	$280,823
Year 9	$9,000	$312,288
Year 10	$9,000	$346,272
Year 11		$382,973
Year 12		$422,611

When you prepare your own plans, draw insight from the steps Nancy took to arrive at the college-funding model. Next, emboldened by her success with investing for college, Nancy decides to tackle her other two largest worries: housing and retirement.

PLAN 2 ▶ *Saving for a Down Payment*

Nancy, who has lived in apartments all her life, hopes to purchase a home in five years. She expects to spend about $200,000 on a property and would prefer to put 20 percent down ($60,000) to lower her mortgage payment and avoid paying private mortgage insurance. Like she did with her daughter's tuition, she decides to boost her target, this time by 20 percent, seeking to come up with $72,000. Assuming she sticks with the 8 percent return target from the college model and has nothing set aside today, how much must she invest each year to have $72,000 available in five years? To accumulate this amount of money, Nancy must save $12,500 per year and earn 8% annually on her investments (see Table 2.5).

This time, Nancy input a zero for her current assets because she had no savings for a down payment. She went with the annual contribution that worked out to $12,000,

TABLE 2.5 SAVING FOR A DOWN PAYMENT		
Annual contribution	$12,500	
Expected returns	8%	
Target	$72,000	
	Investment	Portfolio Value
Current assets	$0	$0
Year 1	$12,500	$12,500
Year 2	$12,500	$26,000
Year 3	$12,500	$40,580
Year 4	$12,500	$56,326
Year 5	$12,500	$73,333

then bumped up the contribution $500 a year so that she could come up with an amount large enough to leave her with more than $72,000 in five years. However, the resulting $12,500 annual investment target was more than she could afford to spend at that moment.

When working out your own numbers, don't consider such findings a failure. After all, knowing you can't afford something will help you avoid ugly mistakes. For example, Nancy can stick with her apartment or scale back her home-buying plans, or she can take on freelance work and boost her income. Having the numbers available in a model will help her weigh the options.

PLAN 3 ▶ *Saving for Retirement*

To calculate how much she must save for retirement, Nancy looks farther into the future. She turns to CNNMoney's retirement calculator for guidance and inputs the relevant numbers as follows:

- *Age*: 35
- *Target retirement age*: 60
- *Amount saved so far*: $200,000
- *Current income*: $100,000 per year

Retirement planning brings concerns beyond those you'll encounter planning for college or most other costs because it involves complicated assumptions about how long you're likely to live and the type of lifestyle you intend to maintain after you stop working. The CNNMoney calculator assumes you'll live to age 92 and takes your income into account, assuming you'll want a comparable standard of living after retirement.

Based on the number Nancy inputs, the retirement calculator estimates she'll need $3.6 million at retirement, a target that takes into account both inflation and an annual growth of 1.5 percent in her salary. The calculator allows for investment planning, but it assumes 6 percent investment returns, so she returns to her Excel sheet. Once again, she plans for the unexpected, bumping up the target by 20 percent to $4.3 million.

Given her desire to pay for her daughter's college, Nancy knows she can't set aside more than $8,000 per year toward retirement. If she retires in 25 years at age 60 with that amount set aside, this model suggests she'd only end up with $1.95 million, less than halfway to her goal of $4.3 million. Working an extra 10 years would get her to the target (see Table 2.6).

If she doesn't want to work an extra 10 years and retire at 70 to make the $4.3 million, Nancy could reduce her spending in other areas and increase her annual investment.

More than the models we've looked at for college tuition and a down payment on a house, the retirement model will require modification. If Nancy abandons plans to buy a house, she could boost her retirement savings. Once she accumulates enough money to put her daughter through college, Nancy can plow the college savings into her retirement as well.

The spreadsheet can handle such life changes. The amount invested just needs to be modified. Hoping for a better result, Nancy adjusts her model to apply the $9,000 she's currently setting aside for college to retirement. Starting in Year 13, she bumps up the investment to $17,000. For good measure, she considers tackling five years of freelance work, which would raise the additional $12,500 a year she'd need to fund the down payment and add it to the retirement pot. Her results? Somewhat disappointing (see Table 2.7).

The investments of $12,500 a year Nancy contributes to her retirement savings for five years in addition to the $9,000 a year she contributes starting in Year 13 will allow her to reach her $4.3 million target in Year 32 at age 67, three years earlier than before.

While the third spreadsheet didn't produce the results Nancy wanted to find, it provided her with a framework for revising her goals. She saw that she could consider more freelance work, cheaper college options, or reductions in her current lifestyle spending to meet her long-haul financial objectives. By modeling plans to invest for college, a house, and retirement, Nancy is determining what she needs and can make intelligent decisions about how to accumulate it.

TABLE 2.6 SAVING FOR RETIREMENT		
Annual contribution	$8,000	
Expected returns	8%	
Target	$4,300,000	
	Investment	Portfolio Value
Current assets	$200,000	$200,000
Year 1	$8,000	$224,000
Year 2	$8,000	$249,920
Year 3	$8,000	$277,914
Year 4	$8,000	$308,147
Year 5	$8,000	$340,798
Year 6	$8,000	$376,062
Year 7	$8,000	$414,147
Year 8	$8,000	$455,279
Year 9	$8,000	$499,701
Year 10	$8,000	$547,677
Year 11	$8,000	$599,492
Year 12	$8,000	$655,451
Year 13	$8,000	$715,887
Year 14	$8,000	$781,158
Year 15	$8,000	$851,651
Year 16	$8,000	$927,783
Year 17	$8,000	$1,010,005
Year 18	$8,000	$1,098,806
Year 19	$8,000	$1,194,710
Year 20	$8,000	$1,298,287
Year 21	$8,000	$1,410,150
Year 22	$8,000	$1,530,962
Year 23	$8,000	$1,661,439
Year 24	$8,000	$1,802,354
Year 25	**$8,000**	**$1,954,543**
Year 26	$8,000	$2,118,906
Year 27	$8,000	$2,296,418
Year 28	$8,000	$2,488,132

TABLE 2.6 SAVING FOR RETIREMENT		
(Table 2.6, continued)	**Investment**	**Portfolio Value**
Year 29	$8,000	$2,695,182
Year 30	$8,000	$2,918,797
Year 31	$8,000	$3,160,301
Year 32	$8,000	$3,421,125
Year 33	$8,000	$3,702,815
Year 34	$8,000	$4,007,040
Year 35	**$8,000**	**$4,335,603**

TABLE 2.7 SAVING FOR RETIREMENT (REVISED)		
Annual contribution	$8,000	
Expected returns	8%	
Target	$4,300,000	
	Investment	**Portfolio Value**
Current assets	$200,000	$200,000
Year 1	$20,500	$236,500
Year 2	$20,500	$275,920
Year 3	$20,500	$318,494
Year 4	$20,500	$364,473
Year 5	$20,500	$414,131
Year 6	$8,000	$455,261
Year 7	$8,000	$499,682
Year 8	$8,000	$547,657
Year 9	$8,000	$599,469
Year 10	$8,000	$655,427
Year 11	$8,000	$715,861
Year 12	$8,000	$781,130
Year 13	$17,000	$860,620
Year 14	$17,000	$946,470
Year 15	$17,000	$1,039,188
Year 16	$17,000	$1,139,323

TABLE 2.7 SAVING FOR RETIREMENT (REVISED)		
(Table 2.7, continued)	Investment	Portfolio Value
Year 17	$17,000	$1,247,469
Year 18	$17,000	$1,364,266
Year 19	$17,000	$1,490,407
Year 20	$17,000	$1,626,640
Year 21	$17,000	$1,773,771
Year 22	$17,000	$1,932,673
Year 23	$17,000	$2,104,287
Year 24	$17,000	$2,289,630
Year 25	**$17,000**	**$2,489,800**
Year 26	$17,000	$2,705,984
Year 27	$17,000	$2,939,463
Year 28	$17,000	$3,191,620
Year 29	$17,000	$3,463,949
Year 30	$17,000	$3,758,065
Year 31	$17,000	$4,075,710
Year 32	**$17,000**	**$4,418,767**

Nancy's adventures highlight the power of the spreadsheet. Save your copy. You can use it to make calculations for just about any financial need. However, although the calculator works well, make sure you understand its weakness—and those of any forecasting model—before you put it to work. No statistical model is better than its weakest estimate. Because we can't predict the future, no estimate is truly safe. The farther out in time the estimate, the greater the risk that the calculator will be wrong.

Suppose you look at a home selling for $150,000 today and hope to buy it in a year. Home prices don't remain constant. However, unless something drastic occurs, the house will probably be worth $140,000 to $160,000 in a year. But what about 20 years from now? If home prices rise at a rate of 2 percent a year, the house will sell for $223,000. However, price gains of 3 percent a year would vault the value of the home to nearly $271,000, while annual increases of 4 percent would send its value above $328,000, more than twice what it's currently worth.

Fortunately, you can take steps to protect yourself from the uncertainty:

- Draw conclusions from the past, as Nancy did when she used historical college-cost inflation to forecast her daughter's future expenses.

WHAT YOU DON'T KNOW ABOUT YOUR RETIREMENT

Maybe you think you're on pace to set aside all you need for your golden years plus have a little cushion. Congratulations, but don't pat yourself on the back just yet.

That "more than you need" can easily transform into "barely enough to make it" or into "way more than you need." Consider the uncertainties inherent in retirement planning.

Having your retirement income exceed your expectations might involve:

- *Underestimating your income by failing to take into account promotions and other income boosts during your prime years at work.* The more you make, the more you are likely to funnel into your retirement portfolio—assuming you don't spend it on other stuff.

- *Paying off your home and then continuing to live in it.* Mortgage expense makes up the largest line item in most people's budgets. Once you pay off your home, the purchasing and investing power of your income may surprise you.

- *Overestimating your postretirement expenses.* Estimates of how much income people will require for retirement vary greatly. Most people's fall within the range of 70 percent to 85 percent of their earnings at the time of retirement, reflecting the reduction in expenses involved in funding a full-time working lifestyle. However, plenty of retirees, particularly those who own their homes outright, can subsist on a lot less than 70 percent of their past earnings.

Having your retirement income fall short could be the result of:

- *Getting sick.* According to Anthony Webb and Natalia Zhivan, a 2010 study by the Center for Retirement Research at Boston College finds that the typical 65-year-old couple can expect to spend $197,000 in today's dollars on health care costs not covered by insurance, with a 5 percent risk of at least $311,000 in costs. Take into account nursing home care, and the typical couple will spend $260,000 with a 5 percent chance of spending more than $570,000.

- *Living longer than you expect.* The blessing of long life can become a curse if you haven't saved up enough money.

- *Facing any number of unexpected expenses.* John Lennon nailed it when he wrote, "Life is what happens to you while you're busy making other plans." Relatives run into financial trouble, homes need repair, politicians take from one group and give to another. That randomness makes retirement planning difficult, and explains why you should overestimate your expenses.

- Use conservative assumptions, as Joe did when he lowered his target return rate to 4 percent.
- Overplan, assuming you'll need more money than expected.

Taken together, these tactics can add muscle to any forecasting model, offering protection against the risk that you've become too optimistic. Worst case, you end up with more money than you need. Most people could live with that kind of inaccuracy.

While time increases the risk inherent in an estimate, don't forget what you learned in chapter 1 about time being an investor's greatest ally. Earlier in this chapter, you read that a $150,000 home appreciating at an annual rate of 2 percent will be worth $223,000 in 20 years, demonstrating time's power. Move out beyond 20 years and the effect magnifies, as shown by table 2.6, Nancy Nickel's first retirement-planning spreadsheet.

During the first 25 years, Nancy's portfolio rose from $200,000 to $1.95 million. And then during the next 10 years, it grew to $4.34 million. In the 35th year alone, the portfolio grew by more than $300,000, dwarfing Nancy's $8,000 investment. Why the massive gains later on in the process? Give the credit to compounding.

Say you invest $10,000 and earn 6 percent. At the end of the year, your portfolio has increased in value by $600 to $10,600. If you were to earn the same 6 percent next year, the portfolio has gained $636—$600 from the 6 percent of the original $10,000 and $36 from the 6 percent of the $600 increase from the previous year. The return earned on past returns adds up over time, amplifying your portfolio gains. Nancy's portfolio gains of $328,000 in Year 35 came mostly from the 8 percent return on the portfolio value of $4 million from Year 34.

The impact of compounding accelerates each year, making a compelling case for an early start to investing. If you read this book at age 25, when you have 40 years until retirement, you'll enjoy far greater options than the 45-year-old reader. However, if you turned 25 a long time ago, don't give up. You can still tap into the benefits of compounding. The sooner you begin, the better the results.

The stock market is filled with individuals who know the price of everything, but the value of nothing.

PHILIP FISHER
AUTHOR OF *COMMON STOCKS AND UNCOMMON PROFITS*

3

KNOW YOUR OPTIONS

Think of the investment market as a restaurant that never runs out of tables. It caters to anyone who finds the front door, and patrons can hang out for as long as they like.

Most eateries feature a few offerings that sell better than the others. The Investment Café boasts a vast menu, with selections designed to please everyone from the casual investor to the person looking specifically to hedge against a rise in the price of the soybeans she plans to buy six months from now. As a rule, individual investors prefer ordering from the biggest names at the top of the menu.

Most Popular Investments

What follows is a sampling of the Investment Café's four most popular entrées: stocks, bonds, mutual funds, and exchange-traded funds.

Stocks

Common stock represents an ownership stake in a company. In the near term, stocks rise and fall in value based on investors' perceptions about the issuing company, the broad stock market, and the economy or other external factors. Stocks trade all day long, and their prices can vary widely intraday as well as from one day to the next. Stock investors must be willing to accept some volatility.

Bonds

When you buy a bond, you purchase a series of interest payments on the debt issued by a company or government entity. Bonds don't provide you with an ownership interest in the company, just the promise of an income stream.

While stocks trade on exchanges that allow investors easy access to pricing data, it takes more work to find bond prices. Not all brokerages buy and sell bonds, and many bonds only sell in denominations too large for the typical investor to acquire a diversified selection. As such, most individuals who seek bond exposure get it through mutual funds.

Mutual Funds

Mutual funds pool the money collected from many investors to purchase a basket of securities that would be tough for individuals to buy on their own. Professional managers oversee the investments for a fee.

Exchange-Traded Funds

Exchange-traded funds (ETFs) operate like mutual funds in that they allow many investors to harness their combined buying power to purchase large amounts of stocks and bonds. However, ETFs trade on exchanges like stocks.

Stocks, bonds, mutual funds, and ETFs provide investors with a range of investment possibilities, from ultraconservative to burn-your-eyebrows-off aggressive. For most individuals who'd rather not put in the time and effort to become investment experts, these four asset classes fill the entire bucket. Those who are more adventurous can venture farther into the wilderness with other types of assets—which you'll learn about a bit later.

Charting a Course

By this point in the book, you have some financial goals in mind, and you know what kinds of investments are out there. In order to parlay that knowledge into meeting and exceeding your long-term financial goals, you need to learn a little more about yourself—specifically which types of investments make the most sense to you.

You might think that once you have a good bead on an investment's characteristics, you'll know whether you should buy it. But suitability for your goals is just one part of the equation. Your investment objectives might require a heavy dose of common stocks.

However, if owning stocks would make you pull your hair out with worry, stay away from them. You must deal with different types of risk. You'll need to balance the risk of failing to achieve your financial objectives against the risk of having a heart

POPULAR INVESTMENTS AT A GLANCE

Stocks

Investment category: growth, possibly income
Risk level: moderate to high
Reward level: moderate to high
Suitability: most investors

Bonds

Investment category: income
Risk level: low to moderate
Reward level: low to moderate
Suitability: only fairly sophisticated investors should purchase individual bonds

Mutual Funds

Investment category: all types
Risk level: all types
Reward level: all types
Suitability: all investors

ETFs

Investment category: all types
Risk level: all types
Reward level: all types
Suitability: all investors

attack before you get to the point in your life when those objectives matter. Investing is a uniquely personal task, and your unique personality will make itself known. Investors who attempt to go against their natural grain—like the thrill seeker trying to avoid risk—often run into trouble when their actions clash with their inclinations.

You can best avoid such destructive conflicts by selecting a path that comes naturally, one that you won't have trouble following. The questionnaire "What Kind of Investor Are You?" at the end of the chapter contains 12 questions designed to slot you into one of nine categories. The goal of the questionnaire isn't to place you into the "best" group. None of the groups has an innate advantage over another. Instead, the quiz will help you find out where on the investment spectrum you live and build a house that suits you. Before you review the categories—before they can sway your thinking in favor of one over another—go do the questionnaire.

Investing Styles

Wall Street has a saying: "Bulls make money, bears make money, pigs get slaughtered." Most of the time, investors break out that adage as a warning that investors who are unprepared tend to do poorly in the market. While the warning makes sense, the first part of the saying also has meaning. Both bulls (those who expect stocks to rise) and bears (those who expect stocks to fall) can do just fine if they select investment strategies that fit their chosen approaches. The same goes for other types of investors.

The questionnaire you just filled out will help you find your tendency in two comparisons of your tolerance for risk. Score 1 rates you on the aggressive/conservative spectrum, while Score 2 gauges your interest in accumulation versus income.

Add up the numbers in the Score 1 column of the questionnaire to gauge your risk tolerance. (In the Investment Purpose section, we will assess Score 2, your preference for income generation versus wealth accumulation.)

- If you scored between 80 and 107, you fall into the aggressive category.
- If you scored between 11 and 40, you qualify as a conservative, at least financially.
- If you scored between 41 and 79, you share both aggressive and conservative traits, which makes you a moderate.

Aggressive investors don't mind taking on risk if the potential returns justify it, while conservatives tend to limit risk. Thrill seekers are by nature aggressive, but they perch at the top of the scale. In contrast, most worriers will find themselves falling toward the conservative end of the spectrum.

Knowing your location on the aggressive/conservative scale can help you avoid common investing mistakes. Each investment style carries its own strengths and weaknesses. In the following pages, you'll learn about pitfalls that tend to catch investors. Not surprisingly, different styles will lead you to different problems.

Aggressive

Aggressive investors probably like stocks more than bonds. They focus on the rewards more than the risk and are likely to take a chance and try an investment they don't know well. If you scored high on the questionnaire, you probably filled your Planning for the Future worksheet with bold goals, including some you don't expect to realize. That willingness to dream can serve you well, as long as you don't let it override your good sense.

As an aggressive investor, you are at greater risk than moderates or conservatives of falling into these three pitfalls:

1. **Impatience.** Investors with an aggressive bent like to make moves. Unfortunately, excessive trading is one of the biggest drags on returns. What you call decisive, others might label foolhardy. After all, you'll pay a commission every time you buy or sell, so the more transactions you make, the more money flows from your account and the more gains you need on the investments to offset those costs. In addition, selling an investment immediately on perceived bad news, as aggressive investors often do, can be a mistake. Often stocks or other securities will decline initially, then rebound after the market has time to correct. Never make an investment decision until you've taken at least a day to sleep on it. Doing so exposes you to more losses if a stock takes a dive on bad news, then dives again the next day. You'll also lessen your chance of bailing out of an investment right before it turns a corner.

- **Young people.** While aggressive investments are riskier, most will deliver superior returns over time. If you have 10 years, or better yet 20 years, feel free to get aggressive—not stupid, but aggressive.

- **Investors who already have money.** The more money you have, the better you can absorb a loss. Wealth can protect you even more than age. Plenty of rich investors set aside enough to live on, then put the rest of their money to work in assets where people of moderate means fear to tread.

- **Experts.** Knowledge and experience can also mitigate risk. Investors who bring expertise to bear and weed out the weak investments from the strong can afford to take more chances. Unfortunately, novice investors who take advice from one of these "experts" will have trouble determining whether she really knows her stuff.

2. **Overconfidence.** As a group, aggressive investors are probably not actually more prideful than any other group. However, before the fall, it is pride that probably causes aggressive investors to hit the ground with the loudest splat. Aggressive investors tend to run ahead of the pack, and it takes confidence to venture where others haven't yet gone. Unfortunately, when you lead the pack, you can't learn from the mistakes of those who went before you. Because of this, aggressive investors need a third party they can trust to serve as a sounding board for investment ideas—and, at times, an emergency brake. Here's a hint: don't select another aggressive investor as your accountability partner or you both may end up driving off the same cliff.

3. **Overconcentration.** Aggressive investors have the tendency to put all of their money into stocks and other high-risk investments in search of the highest returns. But even the youngest, smartest, most optimistic investor in the world shouldn't sink all of her money into these assets and eschew bonds, which tend to underperform stocks over time. Don't fall into that trap. Fixed-income securities such as bonds provide valuable ballast, blunting the risk of portfolios packed with stocks and similar securities. Since stocks and bonds don't always follow the same path, owning a mix of both protects investors during periods when one of the asset classes lags.

Conservative

Conservative investors will find themselves sliding toward bonds and shying away from stocks. Due to holding onto their money, many conservative investors hold more cash than their financial position warrants spending. Their investment style insulates them somewhat from the risk of a truly terrible performance in a given year but exposes them to the greater risk of not meeting their investment objectives.

When it looks like one of her long-term financial goals won't be met, a conservative is more likely to revise the goal than ramp up risk in an effort to boost investment returns. Since you set your own goals, a decision to modify them is just as valid as a decision to ramp up the risk of an investment portfolio in an attempt to juice performance. Investors with an aggressive bent may view such an approach as a capitulation, but the true test involves how the individual feels. If a conservative can come away from his spreadsheet happy that he's scaled back his goals, more power to him.

Conservatives face difficulties specific to them. Here are three common issues:

1. **Underperformance.** You can't argue with this one. Focusing on low-risk securities generally results in a low-return portfolio. Just be honest with yourself. If you intend to concentrate on investments that earn you a 4 percent rather than an 8 percent return, budget with the lower rate in mind. You'll need to set aside more cash on the front end, but slow and steady can win the race, as long as it doesn't forget the steady part.

2. **Complacency.** When conservatives feel safe, they don't want to move. And one of the reasons conservatives stick with low-risk investments revolves around safety. In an environment where others target a 10 percent return and accept the risk of a 10 percent loss if things don't go well, many conservatives bank their 4 percent return in short-term bonds and lean back with their hands behind their heads, comfortable as a pig in slop. Then they wallow in their safety while everyone else earns better returns, and kick themselves a decade later when it becomes apparent they won't reach their long-term goals. Just like aggressive investors, those who acknowledge their own conservatism should find an accountability partner— either another investor or a trusted professional. When that partner brings up a potential problem with your strategy, don't dismiss it. Consider the objections and make a change if needed.

3. **Pessimism.** Don't misread this. A little pessimism is healthy. But too much pessimism can cause you to set your sights low. The personality traits that drive you to conservative investing may conspire to convince you that a goal hovers out of your reach, even if your model suggests you can attain it. Trust your numbers. Of course, you can't simply accept any projection as a guarantee, for a variety of reasons addressed in previous chapters. But since conservatives will tend to over-budget anyway, if the model suggests a path that will reach an important goal, follow that path for a while to see how it works.

WHO SHOULD BE CONSERVATIVE?

- **Investors with short time horizons.** Whether you've saved up enough to cover your financial goal or not, when the purpose for saving that money nears, you must cut back on your risk. Suppose your model suggests you need $1.8 million to retire in two years and you have $1.5 million now. Some investors will feel the pull of an aggressive move, hoping to bridge the gap. But with just two years before retirement, you can't afford to risk much of your principal. Two bad years in the market (always a risk, even for the best investors) could set you back big time. Instead, you might consider reducing your spending plans to live on what you already have. The shorter the time between now and when you need the money, the less risk you can afford to take with that money.

- **Investors who already have money.** If you recognize this one from the section on aggressive investment style, your memory hasn't failed you. Once again, wealth provides flexibility. Yes, the wealthy can afford to take risks. But they can also afford to avoid risk if they choose.

- **Anyone with no stomach for volatility.** Some investment decisions ignore the rational part of your brain that calculates how much you need and when you need it. Rich or poor, old or young, if deviating from a conservative approach will cost you sleep, then stick to what comes naturally. Better to adjust your lifestyle in other areas. No investment is good enough to put your health at risk.

Moderate

If you scored in the moderate range on your questionnaire, don't equate that with being wishy-washy. By avoiding the extremes in either direction, you probably have an easier time tailoring your investment portfolio to your financial situation. When a goal seems out of reach, a moderate investor will calmly consider whether a move to higher-return investments makes sense, without taking on more risk. Consider a moderate investment approach as a balanced diet.

While moderation provides plenty of advantages for investors, no approach is bulletproof. Beware of the following three traps:

1. **Market matching.** By nature, investors with both aggressive and conservative habits will skew to the middle of the investment pack. The first won't suffer the embarrassing lows of investors who tend to make big bets in one direction and get caught pants down when the market shifts. The other won't share in the glorious profits that come when an extremist makes the right call at the right time.

If you don't mind that your returns will rarely be among the tops in a given year, you won't need a lifeline. There's nothing wrong with earning a string of Bs rather than a blend of As and Cs with the occasional D. However, if you'd rather try for stronger returns regardless of market conditions, you'll need to distinguish yourself via your selection of individual investments. In other words, either become a talented picker of stocks and bonds or hook up with someone who is.

2. **Laziness.** When you don't sway with the whims of the market, you can easily get used to sitting back and watching the pendulum swing. While this is not a bad approach if you can pull it off, sometimes markets undergo massive, destabilizing shifts. Examples include the massive bull market of the late 1990s, the crash of 2000, and the financial crisis that got rolling in 2008. Each of those three events sparked a multiyear period when stocks and bonds deviated from typical patterns. So be willing to get more aggressive when markets stay weak for long periods and to pull in your horns when rallies start to look long in the tooth. Of course, such advice always comes with a caveat: Timing market moves is difficult; even the experts don't get it right all the time.

3. **Indecisiveness.** While a moderate stance can keep you from acting irrationally, it can also hinder you when decision time arrives. The very lack of extremism that benefits a moderate investor by not pulling her down a dangerous path can also leave her somewhat insensitive to external forces, and thus slow to act. Pay close attention to the financial news as well as news involving the companies in which you've invested. This is good advice for any investor, but doubly so for those who aren't already sensitive to imbalances.

Investment Purpose

The set of scores in the second column of the questionnaire attempts to determine whether you invest for wealth accumulation or for income. Of course, people invest for other reasons as well. But most securities are designed to either rise in value over time, pay out income, or a combination of both.

Add up the numbers in the Score 2 column of the questionnaire to gauge your preference for wealth accumulation versus income.

- If you scored between 60 and 84, you prefer to invest for income.
- Scores between 10 and 35 suggest you'd rather focus on building wealth.
- Scores between 36 and 59 don't show much of a preference for income over accumulation, or vice versa.

A focus on income often goes hand in hand with a conservative investment approach, in large part because many of the factors that cause an investor to be conservative—a short time horizon, low risk tolerance, and the need to fund a

TABLE 3.1 NINE TYPES OF INVESTORS			
		Score 2	
		10–35	36–59	60–84
Score 1	11–40	Aggressive, Preference for Income	Moderate, Preference for Income	Conservative, Preference for Income
	41–79	Aggressive, Neutral on Accumulation versus Income	Moderate, Neutral on Accumulation versus Income	Conservative, Neutral on Accumulation versus Income
	80–107	Aggressive, Preference for Accumulation	Moderate, Preference for Accumulation	Conservative, Preference for Accumulation

retirement lifestyle—make income-generating investments more appealing. Bonds, which deliver most of their returns via income, are more conservative than stocks.

Still, plenty of investors with an aggressive mindset would like to derive income from their portfolios, while some conservative investors don't need the income and would prefer to grow their wealth—safely, of course.

Finding Your Niche

The combination of three investment styles and three investment purposes makes for nine types of investors. Check out the Table 3.1 to determine what type of investor you are, based on your totals for Score 1 and Score 2. Of course, none of these labels is an absolute, as few people follow the same approach for everything. Many of you probably scored near the border between one category and another, which means you exhibit characteristics of both categories and shouldn't limit yourself to a narrow interpretation of what is appropriate.

Regardless of your position on the investment spectrum, start the investment process by considering the nature of the investment and whether it will help you meet your goals. After you've determined an investment seems to make sense, then consider whether it fits your investment approach.

WHAT KIND OF INVESTOR ARE YOU?

For each question, circle the most appropriate description in the first column of the questionnaire. Then place the corresponding numbers in the Risk Tolerance and Income Generation vs. Wealth Accumulation score columns to the right. When you are done with all 12 questions, add up the scores in each column and write the sum at the bottom of the table in the Total row. You will go on to use the two numbers to assess your investment style.

Question 1: How much time are you willing to devote to seeking, analyzing, and following investments every week?			
		Risk tolerance	Income generation vs. wealth accumulation
No time	(RT = 0; IG = –)		
Up to 1 hour	(RT = 3; IG = –)		
1–3 hours	(RT = 5; IG = –)		
3–5 hours	(RT = 7; IG = –)		
More than 5 hours	(RT = 10; IG = –)		
Question 2: What would you like your investments to do?			
		Risk tolerance	Income generation vs. wealth accumulation
Increase in value	(RT = 8; IG = 0)		
Increase in value and provide income, but value is more important	(RT = 6; IG = 3)		
Increase in value and provide income, with both equally important	(RT = 5; IG = 5)		
Increase in value and provide income, but income is more important	(RT = 4; IG =7)		
Provide income	(RT = 2; IG =10)		
Question 3: Think of your single most important investment goal. How far in the future will you need that money?			
		Risk tolerance	Income generation vs. wealth accumulation
Less than 2 years	(RT = 2; IG = 8)		
2–5 years	(RT = 5; IG = 6)		
6–10 years	(RT = 8; IG = 4)		
11 years or more	(RT = 10; IG = 2)		

WHAT KIND OF INVESTOR ARE YOU?

Question 4: How many more years do you intend to work before retirement?

		Risk tolerance	Income generation vs. wealth accumulation
5 years or less	(RT = 10; IG = 10)		
6–10 years	(RT = 7; IG = 7)		
11–20 years	(RT = 5; IG = 3)		
21–30 years	(RT = 3; IG = 1)		
More than 30 years	(RT= 0; IG = 0)		

Question 5: What is your level of knowledge about investments?

		Risk tolerance	Income generation vs. wealth accumulation
None	(RT = 1; IG = –)		
Limited	(RT = 3; IG = –)		
Moderate	(RT = 5; IG = –)		
Good	(RT = 7; IG = –)		
Extensive	(RT = 9; IG = –)		

Question 6: What kind of investments do you own or have you owned in the past? If more than one answer applies, select the option with the highest number of points.

		Risk tolerance	Income generation vs. wealth accumulation
Cash or money-market investments	(RT = 0; IG = –)		
Bond mutual funds	(RT = 2; IG = –)		
Individual bonds	(RT = 3; IG = –)		
U.S. stocks or stock mutual funds	(RT = 6; IG = –)		
International stocks or mutual funds	(RT = 8; IG = –)		
Stock options or other derivatives	(RT = 10; IG = –)		

Question 7: Suppose your financial adviser presents you with the five investment options in the following chart. Which would you prefer?

	Likely annual return	Worst-case return	Best-case return
A	4%	1%	7%
B	5.50%	0%	11%
C	9%	–5%	23%
D	12%	–15%	40%
E	12%	–25%	53%

WHAT KIND OF INVESTOR ARE YOU?			

Question 7, *continued*

		Risk tolerance	Income generation vs. wealth accumulation
A	(RT = 1; IG = 10)		
B	(RT = 3; IG = 8)		
C	(RT = 5; IG = 5)		
D	(RT = 8; IG = 3)		
E	(RT = 10; IG = 1)		

Question 8: Which statement best describes your attitude toward money?			
		Risk tolerance	Income generation vs. wealth accumulation
"I can't stand to see my investments lose value."	(RT = 1; IG = 8)		
"I don't worry too much about the value of my investments as long as they keep paying dividends."	(RT = 3; IG = 10)		
"I'm willing to accept some risk of loss, but only if there's a good chance for gain."	(RT = 5; IG = 5)		
"You can't make money without taking risks."	(RT = 8; IG = 2)		

Question 9: Which statement best describes your attitude about profits and losses?			
		Risk tolerance	Income generation vs. wealth accumulation
"After I lose a little money on an investment, I'm ready to stop taking risks and trying to make a profit."	(RT = 0; IG = 9)		
"I dislike losing money more than I like making money."	(RT = 3; IG = 7)		
"I like making money about equal to the amount I dislike losing money."	(RT = 5; IG = 5)		
"I like making money more than I dislike losing money."	(RT = 7; IG = 3)		
"I don't mind losing money if I have a chance to make it up in the future."	(RT = 9; IG = 1)		

WHAT KIND OF INVESTOR ARE YOU?

Question 10: How would you rate your current level of wealth?

		Risk tolerance	Income generation vs. wealth accumulation
High	(RT = 7; IG = 1)		
Fairly high	(RT = 5; IG = 3)		
Moderate	(RT = 6; IG = 5)		
Fairly low	(RT = 4; IG = 7)		
Low	(RT = 3; IG = 9)		

Question 11: Suppose you owned a stock that lost 15 percent of its value in a three-month period. The broad stock market also fell 15 percent in the same period. What would you do?

		Risk tolerance	Income generation vs. wealth accumulation
Sell all of my shares and cut my losses	(RT = 1; IG = 8)		
Sell some of my shares and reduce my bet	(RT = 3; IG = 7)		
Nothing	(RT = 5; IG = 5)		
Buy more shares	(RT = 8; IG = 3)		

Question 12: What is the number one reason I want to invest?

				Risk tolerance	Income generation vs. wealth accumulation
To build my wealth	a	b	(a = 10; b = 0)		
To boost my income	a	b	(a = 5; b = 10)		
To make me and/or my family feel safer	a	b	(a = 0; b = 5)		
TOTAL					

In a bull market, one must avoid the error of the preening duck that quacks boastfully after a torrential rainstorm, thinking that its paddling skills have caused it to rise in the world. A right-thinking duck would instead compare its position after the downpour to that of the other ducks on the pond.

WARREN BUFFETT
CHAIRMAN OF BERKSHIRE HATHAWAY, 1997 LETTER TO SHAREHOLDERS

4

KNOW YOUR LIMITS

Warren Buffett would rather not buy stock. His company, Berkshire Hathaway, owns about 9 percent of Coca-Cola—a stake worth more than $15 billion at the end of March 2014—making it Coke's largest shareholder. When possible, Buffett prefers to purchase the entire company, not just a piece. It's a nice strategy if you can write a check with eight zeroes. Unfortunately, very few people have that option.

Yes, you must invest. But if you commit more money than you can afford, you set yourself up for disaster if your selected investments don't rise in value and keep rising steadily. Few investments do that. Check out a stock chart. Even the best-performing stocks will take a step back for every two steps forward. This doesn't mean the company will implode. Investors with time and patience can benefit from waiting out a strong company's weak patches. However, the "have patience" strategy only works if you can personally afford to hold on through the rough times, or even take a loss periodically when your investment craps out. Sometimes even the best-researched, most attractive securities will disappoint you.

Every good investor knows she'll make some bad decisions. Success comes not from being right all the time but from getting enough calls right to more than offset the inevitable stinkers—which brings the issue back to living within your means.

The Variety of Income Types

If you invest only as much as you can afford, a near-term setback won't knock you off your feet. As for what you can afford, that depends in large part on what you bring in. Most income falls into three categories—earned income, investment income, and passive income. At least at first, novice investors can tap into only one of them.

Earned Income

As the words imply, you earn this money by working. Salaries, commissions, consulting fees, business income—all of those sources of cash fall under the umbrella of earned income.

The good thing is, pretty much everyone can earn at least a little income. The more training and expertise you bring to the table, the more you can potentially earn. But even workers with little to offer can generally make a few bucks doing unskilled jobs. And regardless of the work you do, over time you can usually increase your earning potential by learning new skills or putting in more hours.

Chief advantages:

- You don't need money to get started. Just time and a willingness to work.
- As long as you hold a job, the money keeps rolling in.
- These funds allow you to build wealth, paving the way to the other two types of income.

Chief disadvantages:

- Every dollar takes time to earn. While you can probably boost your income by working longer, there are only so many hours in the day.
- When you stop working, the money flow dries up. This seems obvious, but given that the change in financial status from earner to nonearner has spawned an entire industry that revolves around retirement planning, the statement must be made.
- Investing time and effort into education and training might boost your income, but it might not. When you earn income, someone else determines how much to pay you, and that someone might disagree with your assessment of your own worth.

Investment Income

You generate this type of income by selling securities for more than you paid for them or by collecting interest or dividends paid by the securities. This book focuses primarily on stocks, bonds, and funds that contain those securities. Stocks pay dividends while bonds pay interest, and you can sell both for a profit (or a loss).

Chief advantages:

- Investment income can benefit from compounding, as you reinvest what you've already earned.
- If you sell assets after holding them for more than a year, you'll usually pay a lower tax rate than that levied on earned income.

INVESTING WITHIN YOUR MEANS

Invest as much as you can but no more. To determine how much you can afford to invest, learn about your financial condition and start managing your money effectively before putting it anywhere near a brokerage account. Here are five tips to help you figure out how much you should plow into your investments:

1. **Budget your money.** Record how much you make and how much you spend every month. Not for the average of the last six months, or the perfect month, or the month when someone sends you a check you didn't expect, but every single month. Track your income and expenses, and make sure you spend every dime on purpose. Consumer advocate Dave Ramsey likes to say that if you don't tell your money where to go, you'll wonder where it went. If you don't already have a budget, turn to page 54 for a sample budget worksheet.

2. **Take a little off the top.** Before you start paying bills, and before you dip below the top lines of your budget, set aside a slice of the cash to invest. This may sound counterintuitive, because at least in the near term, skipping a mortgage payment because you invested the money will hurt you more than shortchanging your retirement fund. However, if you maintain a budget, you'll know how much you can invest. By setting that money aside before you start spending the rest, you know it will still be ready to work for you after the bills go into the mail. If, on the other hand, you cover the rest of the costs first, your investment funds may disappear in a wave of fast-food lunches and Friday-night movies. Treat investment spending like a crucial bill and allocate it before you spend a dime on anything discretionary.

3. **Take advantage of retirement plans.** If your employer offers a tax-advantaged retirement plan like a 401(k), and especially if it matches a portion of your contributions, get involved. Many investors get their first taste of the financial markets via employer-sponsored retirement plans. These plans offer a number of benefits, including making the investment automatic so you don't have to exercise the discipline to set money aside every paycheck.

4. **Don't overdo it.** Sometimes your investment model says you'd better start deploying 25 percent of your income for retirement or you'll end up eating dog food for breakfast and pork and beans for dinner. The numbers probably aren't lying, but don't move up to huge investments right away. Work through your budget to determine how much you can afford to invest while still leaving enough to pay for necessities plus a small amount of frills to keep you from going crazy. Over time, you can modify your budget and boost the retirement you set aside to the levels you need.

5. **Live cheaply.** If your budget doesn't include room for the level of investing you seek, cut back on spending. Or increase your disposable income by earning more. If you're like most people, you'll find it easier to change what goes out than what comes in. Need help? You can find advice and support at websites such as Daveramsey.com, Stretcher.com, Feedthepig.org, and Thesimpledollar.com.

- Once you've built a portfolio, it works for you all day, every day. The income it generates often has little connection to how many hours you work and in fact will continue to earn after you stop working and your earned income dries up.

Chief disadvantages:

- Market downturns can erode the value of your portfolio, and you can't work extra hours or look for another job to turn the tide.
- You don't run the companies in which you invest but instead must trust the executives in charge to make decisions that will cause your portfolio to increase in value. Sometimes, they'll do something stupid and cost you money.
- You must pay to play. Without an up-front commitment of cash, you can't acquire wealth-building assets. While compounding will boost returns over time, you may not reap many gains in the near term until you've invested a substantial amount.

Passive Income

This type of income is the most elusive but probably the best overall in terms of what you receive relative to what you put in. Passive income flows from assets that you own but don't spend much time to operate.

For example, you might purchase a business and hire someone to run it, collecting a piece of the profits. Other types of passive income include royalties on intellectual property and income from real estate—assuming you don't manage the property yourself.

Chief advantages:

- Most investments that yield passive income require an ownership interest. While you may not spend much time operating the business, you do have some influence over how others run it, allowing for more control than you'll have with portfolio investments.
- The types of investments that generate passive income generally have staying power, in the form of either long-term leases or continuing business operations. In other words, you'll keep making money for some time, probably with less fluctuation in value than financial investments provide.
- In many cases, passive income receives preferential tax treatment because you can deduct expenses incurred while generating it.

Chief disadvantages:

- The types of assets that generate an income stream without requiring the owner to put in time to operate a business generally cost quite a bit of money to get started. You can build up an investment portfolio gradually over time, but most sources of passive income don't work that way.

- Many sources of passive income are complex, requiring substantial expertise to understand. Just because you inherited $5 million and used it to purchase a widget factory doesn't mean you know anything about widgets or would recognize the danger signs if the business runs into trouble.

The Income Path

Most people rely on earned income when they start their adult life, and without that salary, they can't build up to investment income or passive income. The core purpose of investing is to generate wealth beyond what your earned income can provide, either to supplement that income and purchase a better lifestyle or to fund future expenses your paycheck can't cover on its own. Use your budget to determine how much you can afford to invest. Then make the commitment to invest those funds and increase them as your earnings rise over time.

Budgets reflect your present circumstances and don't rely on financial models and future estimates. If your earned income doesn't provide enough to fund your current lifestyle and also invest for longer-term goals, you can make changes now to reduce your spending or alter your long-term plans. Modifying your current spending is a simpler process than committing to changes in an uncertain future.

Making a Budget

The categories in Worksheet 4.1 represent expenses common to many individuals. You probably won't use all of the lines on this sample budget, and you may wish to create other lines that suit your situation. As a rule of thumb, any expense that eats up at least 5 percent of your take-home pay should have its own line item in the budget.

Start by filling in your income for one pay period. Record your take-home pay; then subtract absolutely nonnegotiable expenses (investing belongs in this section) to calculate your spendable income. Below Spendable Income, in the Expenses section, fill in the amount of your bills and living expenses.

Maintain a running balance as you subtract expenses. After you account for everything—including money spent on pizza or movie rentals or that new bowling ball you just had to have—add up your total expenses and subtract them from Spendable Income. Then record any excess money in the Surplus row and transfer it to the top of the column for the next pay period.

Don't forget, it's okay to blow money if you can afford to. Just do it on purpose and record it on the budget so you can look back and see where all the money went.

You can use the worksheet to track your expenses to see where the budget missed the mark and adjust accordingly. If you spent $150 on gas during each of the last three pay periods, the $100 you budgeted won't cut it. Beef up the gasoline allocation, reducing one or more of the other lines by a similar amount.

WORKSHEET 4.1 BLANK BUDGET

Income/expense category	Monthly amount
Take-home pay	
Tithes	
Alimony/child support	
Investments	
Spendable Income	$0
Expenses	
Bills	
Rent	
Gas and electric	
Telephone	
Mobile phone	
Water and sewer	
Auto insurance	
Cable	
Car payment	
Credit card payment	
Living Expenses	
Groceries	
Dining out	
Gasoline	
Clothing	
Entertainment	
Miscellaneous	
Total Expenses	$0
Surplus	$0

Don't worry if the budget doesn't work at first. They never do, but time and experience will win out. After recording your budget three or four pay periods, you should have a decent handle on what you spend relative to what you bring in as well as reasonable estimates of how much you should be spending in each category. At that point, you can determine how much to invest.

Of course, none of this will work unless you commit to living on the budget you create. If you allocate $50 a month to entertainment and blow it all during the first week, then you have to make an effort not to spend a dime on entertainment until the next pay period. That may not sound like fun, but it pays off. Live by your budget

WORKSHEET 4.2 JOE INVESTOR'S BUDGET						
Income/expense category	Monthly amount	Due date	Jan. 1		Jan. 15	
Balance				$500		$340
Take-home pay	$4,000		$2,000	$2,500	$2,000	$2,340
Tithes	$500		$250	$2,250	$250	$2,090
Investments	$500		$250	$2,000	$250	$1,840
Available to spend	$3,000			$2,000		$1,840
Expenses						
Bills						
Rent	$1,000	15th	$1,000	$1,000		$1,840
Gas and electric	$140	8th	$140	$860		$1,840
Mobile phone	$100	27th		$860	$100	$1,740
Water and sewer	$20	1st		$860	$20	$1,720
Auto insurance	$120	19th	$120	$740		$1,720
Video service	$20	3rd		$740	$20	$1,700
Car payment	$500	22nd		$740	$500	$1,200
Credit-card payment	$300	21st		$740	$300	$900
Living expenses						
Groceries	$220		$110	$630	$110	$790
Dining out	$50		$25	$605	$25	$765
Gasoline	$400		$200	$405	$200	$565
Clothing	$30		$15	$390	$15	$550
Entertainment	$50		$25	$365	$25	$525
Household	$50		$25	$340	$25	$500
Total Expenses	$3,000					

and you won't spend your retirement nest egg on tickets for a movie you'll forget by next month.

In Worksheet 4.2, you'll find an example of a budget in action. Joe Investor created this budget to account for his income and expenses. He starts out with the $500 you see at the top of the column for January 1, which he got from his Christmas bonus. Joe takes home $2,000 every two weeks and immediately takes out funds for his nonnegotiable expenses. He doesn't pay alimony, but he does tithe on his income and put some money toward his investments. Such costs warrant their own section of the budget.

While the budget is a financial document, never let finance crowd out the ethical or legal responsibilities that drive your life. If you tithe for religious reasons or pay child support, cutting those costs to make a budget work could end up causing you more grief than the amount of money you save is worth.

Below the section for nonnegotiables, Joe allocates funds to cover his bills, based on when they come due. At the bottom of his budget, he allocates funds for living expenses.

Joe ends the Jan. 1 pay period with $340 left after covering expenses, then starts the next pay period by adding $340 to the top. While you can't use Joe's budget, you can certainly modify the format to fit your needs, swapping out Joe's income and expenses and changing categories if needed.

PART II

Investment Types

MASTERING THE NUANCES OF
RISKS AND REWARDS

B y now, you understand how and why to invest. If you filled out the worksheets in the earlier chapters, you also have a good idea of how much you'll need at the end of the process as well as how much you must set aside now to reach your goal. In this section of the book, you'll learn more about the nature of the investments themselves and how to make the most of them.

Remember that investments are like attack dogs. If you learn the proper commands and treat them well, they'll fight to protect your interests. But for the foolish person who attempts to control such a dog without the proper training or discipline—well, people have lost more than fingers by doing that.

Every investment comes with its own mix of risks and rewards. As the investor in command of the pack, it's your responsibility to master the nuances. After all, these securities don't come with a user's manual. Consider this chapter of the book as the manual you're going to use.

Every once in a while, the market does something

so stupid it takes your breath away.

JIM CRAMER

BEST-SELLING AUTHOR AND HOST OF *CNBC'S MAD MONEY*,
CO-FOUNDER AND CHAIRMAN OF THESTREET.COM INC.

5

A WALK THROUGH WALL STREET

If you've ever read the *Wall Street Journal* or taken part in a financial discussion of any sort, you've heard Wall Street mentioned. The term refers to a physical location in New York's Financial District that served as the original home of the New York Stock Exchange. Over the years, Wall Street has become a proxy for the financial markets themselves, and for the stock exchanges, banks, and brokerages that administer those markets.

In the information age, you need not visit Wall Street, or even New York City, to participate in the markets. Stocks, bonds, and mutual funds trade through brokers—individuals or firms who charge investors commissions in exchange for executing transactions. In most cases, they allow investors to buy and sell over the Internet. Traditional brokers can easily handle stocks and fund purchases.

Many stocks and all exchange-traded funds (ETFs) trade on exchanges, marketplaces designed to support the buying and selling of financial instruments. Investors in most parts of the world can make trades on exchanges by using their brokers as intermediaries.

While investors can purchase many mutual funds and all ETFs through brokers, most fund companies also have accounts that can be set up by individuals, bypassing the broker. Bonds require a bit more work. Most individual bonds trade over the counter (OTC). The OTC market consists of investment companies, brokers, banks, and dealers with an inventory of bonds. Thousands of stocks also trade through OTC markets.

Expect to pay higher commissions and jump through a few more hoops to purchase individual bonds. However, once you find a broker who can handle the trades, you shouldn't have much trouble—the selection is huge.

Most bonds sell in $5,000 denominations, putting them out of reach for smaller investors who can't afford to concentrate that amount of money in a single investment. As a result, bond funds are popular, allowing investors to buy smaller pieces of a large number of bonds.

While buying these investments is as simple as setting up an account and paying for the purchase, the process of deciding what to buy requires far more thought. Which investments make the most sense for you personally? Read on to find out.

Common Stocks

Each share of common stock gives an investor a stake in a company. For example, technology giant IBM has about a billion shares outstanding. That means for each share you purchase, you own about one-billionth of IBM, which entitles you to a share of the stock's profits and dividends. Does this mean you can call up IBM and ask the company to send you one-billionth of its income for the last year? Not at all. You own a piece of the company, but you don't operate that company. IBM's management will decide how to spend its money, which projects to pursue, and how much of its cash to pay out to shareholders in the form of dividends.

Over time, the three biggest determinants of stock prices are corporate profits, interest rates, and inflation. All else equal, stocks benefit from low inflation, low-to-moderate interest rates, and rising corporate profits.

Do not confuse common stocks with preferred stocks. Preferred stocks don't provide an equity stake in their issuing company and tend to behave more like bonds.

PROS

- **Flexibility.** Stocks trade all day long, allowing investors to choose when to buy and sell.
- **Liquidity.** Exchanges allow most stocks to be bought and sold quickly. Some stocks of tiny companies, or those with extremely high prices, don't trade very often. But you can conduct a transaction for most stocks whenever you like.
- **Variety.** At the end of 2012, nearly 5,000 stocks traded on U.S. exchanges, with hundreds more available in OTC markets. The companies represented cover all facets of the economy, allowing investors to tap into pretty much any industry.
- **Performance.** From 1926 through 2013, large-company stocks have delivered annualized returns of 10.1 percent and small-company stocks 12.3 percent. Both of those returns dwarf what bonds have managed.
- **Limitless growth.** Theoretically, stocks have no upper limit on their value. Giants such as Apple, ExxonMobil, and Procter & Gamble started out as much

smaller companies. If you identify a winner, it might rise to 10 times its original value or more. Such massive gains are rare, but they do happen.

- **Research.** Investors can access a wealth of data on stocks, mostly in the form of information provided free of charge from multiple sources online. Publicly traded companies must file financial reports with the Securities and Exchange Commission in which they provide far more details than most investors can use. Analysts publish estimates for company sales and profits. Companies issue news releases talking about themselves and their products. Not every company generates a lot of news, but you can find something about any firm that interests you.
- **Taxes.** Capital gains—rises in the price of a stock—are generally taxed at a lower rate than earned income. If you hold the assets for more than a year, you'll pay an even-lower long-term rate.

CONS

- **Volatility.** Stock prices can fluctuate wildly. Remember those strong returns in the Pros section? They come at the risk of much greater volatility than bonds.
- **Losses.** While neither bonds nor funds guarantee a positive return, stocks create even more concern for individual investors. Unless a company fails to pay back its bonds, an investor knows she will at least receive her principal back when the bond matures. Mutual funds can adjust to changing markets by selling some securities and buying others. Individual stocks, on the other hand, provide no guarantees to investors.
- **Randomness.** Stock prices can frustrate even the most experienced investor. Sometimes they'll rise or fall on no apparent news or despite news that seems like it should drive them in the opposite direction.
- **Subordination.** If a company happens to go under, stockholders are brought to the table last. In most cases, the company must satisfy its suppliers, pay its employees, and resolve its debts to bondholders before those who own common stock receive a piece of the assets.
- **Outside influence.** While stocks tend to rise and fall along with the fortunes of the company over time, outside forces the company cannot control also wield influence. Sometimes the government will raise tax rates on an industry or increase regulation. Sometimes a foreign competitor will flood the market with cheaper goods and undercut a company. And sometimes a shift in interest rates or currency exchange will take a bite out of a stock's operating results.
- **Groupthink.** When one group of stocks declines, others often follow, even if the factors that drove the first group down don't affect the rest. If the broad stock market declines 10 percent, your stock may suffer the same decline even if it continues to grow its sales and increase its profitability. In other words, your stock may get caught up in a stampede you can't anticipate or avoid.

WHO SHOULD BUY STOCKS?

Individual stocks vary greatly in risk. But as a group, stocks are riskier than bonds. Because stocks offer higher long-term returns than bonds, most investors will need to hold some stocks in order to achieve their investment goals. As such, every investor should own some. However, stocks will generally appeal more to aggressive and moderate investors than to conservatives.

While price appreciation has accounted for the bulk of stock returns over the last 30 years, plenty of stocks pay dividends. Stocks make sense to both investors seeking to accumulate wealth and those who need income. However, using stocks as an income source has drawbacks:

- As of June 9, 2014, the average stock in the S&P 500 Index paid a yield of 1.8 percent, which means the average stock distributed a dividend equivalent to 1.8 percent of its share price. And while more than 400 of the large caps in that index pay dividends, a far-lower percentage of small stocks have dividends. As a group, stocks offer far less income potential than bonds.

- Most of the highest-yielding stocks are concentrated in a few corners of the market—financial companies, real estate investment trusts, energy partnerships, telecommunications companies, and a few other groups—making it difficult to assemble a diversified portfolio of stocks that pay generous dividends. The tight industry groupings needed to generate high yields make for a riskier investment.

- If a company runs into trouble, it can stop paying a stock dividend at will. Sure, it will pay a public-relations price. But because they aren't obligated to pay dividends on their stocks, companies can make the cut if needed. Failing to pay a bond dividend represents default on the debt, with nastier side effects than omitting a stock dividend. As such, if a company needs to cut back a payment to preserve cash, stock dividends are more vulnerable targets, as many investors who owned bank stocks before the financial crisis can attest.

Bonds

Bond buyers are, in effect, loaning money to a company. In exchange for an up-front payment to purchase the bond, investors receive a series of interest payments until the bond matures, at which point the company that issued the bond repays the debt.

Suppose Acme Flatware wants to build a new factory so it can expand into the napkin market. It might fund the $50 million project by issuing 10-year bonds. Investors pay the $50 million up front, and Acme uses the cash to build its factory. Over the course of the next 10 years, Acme makes semiannual interest payments to the investors. At the end of 10 years, the company pays back the $50 million, returning the bondholders' initial investment.

Bonds are broadly classified as fixed-income investments, though not all bonds provide a fixed payment, and they tend to appeal to those who need their investment portfolios to generate cash income.

Bonds rise and fall in value, but not as quickly or easily as stocks. While a stock can double in price if a company's profits grow and its business strengthens, such a change in a company's operating status shouldn't have much of an effect on bond prices. Of more importance is the prevailing interest rate. When rates fall and new bonds of comparable quality can't match the interest rate paid by the older bond, the price should rise. On the other hand, when rates rise and investors can easily lend to new borrowers at a higher rate than the existing bond pays, the bond's price usually falls.

In addition, the fact that the issuer will eventually repay the bond at its issue price limits how high that bond can rise in value and how far it can fall. If you invested $10,000 five years ago and know you'll get that $10,000 back five years from now when the bond matures, how much can you expect someone to pay for the bond today, even if it generates a higher yield than the market? Five years from now, no matter the state of interest rates or inflation or the economy, that bond will revert to a value of $10,000.

PROS

- **Size.** As measured by the total market value of all outstanding securities, the U.S. bond market has been bigger than the U.S. stock market in 25 of the last 26 years. Stocks command more headlines, but the bond market's breadth accommodates any investor interested in making a purchase.
- **Variety.** Bonds come in many types, each with characteristics that add something different to a portfolio. The most common types follow:
  - *Treasury bonds*: They are technically considered default proof.
  - *Corporate bonds*: They allow exposure to all facets of the U.S. economy.
  - *Municipal bonds*: Interest on debt issued by states, municipalities, and quasi-governmental entities is exempt from federal income taxes.
  - *High-yield bonds (also called junk bonds)*: Rated below investment grade, these bonds offer higher yields as compensation for higher risk.
  - *Asset-backed bonds*: These securities created from loans taken out to purchase assets such as houses or cars.
  - *Convertible bonds*: They can transform into stock under certain circumstances.
  - *Zero-coupon bonds*: They trade at a deep discount from their face value. They don't pay interest, but at maturity they are redeemed for face value, with a result much like a stock that increased in price.
  - *Variable-rate bonds*: Their interest payments rise and fall along with the prevailing interest rate. While bonds are characterized as fixed-income investments, not all types of bonds satisfy the description.

- **Flexibility.** Bonds can be purchased that mature anywhere from less than a year to more than 20 years in the future, allowing for a panorama of risk and return levels. In addition, many bonds come with options that change their characteristics over time.
- **Variability of income levels.** Depending on the maturity of the bond and the credit risk of the issuer, investors can choose bonds with a wide range of income levels. In general, higher-income bonds equate to higher risk, but even higher-yielding junk bonds are considered less risky than most stocks.
- **Priority.** In the event a company declares bankruptcy, bondholders have priority over stockholders. In such worst-case scenarios, a company might have almost no assets, leaving everyone high and dry. But when the bankrupt company still has assets, bondholders will get paid back before stockholders.
- **Predictability.** Some bond payouts vary over time. Most provide a reliable income stream that won't change just because of changes in the economy or business climate. While bond prices rise and fall based on changes in interest rates, the payout remains constant, and investors who hold the bond to maturity don't have to worry about price fluctuations, because they know they'll get their money back in the end. In an uncertain market, that kind of consistency has value.
- **Ratings.** Bonds carry credit ratings that reflect their risk of default and allow investors to customize the risk of their bond portfolios. Standard & Poor's assigns AAA ratings to the highest-quality bonds, with the scale sliding back from AA and A to BBB. Any bond rated BBB or above is considered investment grade. Bonds rated BB or lower are called junk bonds. Two other companies—Moody's Investors Services and Fitch—also provide ratings. In general, the lower the rating, the higher the interest the bond must pay to compensate investors for the risk.

CONS

- **Complexity.** The very versatility that makes bonds so useful also makes them intimidating. For the investor who simply wants a fixed-income complement to her stock holdings, which bond makes the most sense? Unfortunately, that question rarely has a simple, definable answer.
- **Returns.** Investment returns can fluctuate substantially from year to year. However, over long periods of time bonds have underperformed stocks. Since 1926, long-term corporate bonds have at times managed annualized returns of 6 percent, while long-term treasuries have delivered around 5.5 percent. Over that same period, treasury bills sometimes notched an annualized return of 3.5 percent, barely enough to offset inflation (3 percent). If your investment goals require a long-term return of more than 5 percent, you'll need some stocks to make it work. If you target returns of 8 percent or more, you'll need a heavy dose of stocks, taking on the commensurate risk.

WHO SHOULD BUY BONDS?

Bonds are best known for the income they provide. Interest payments aren't guaranteed, but as long as the company remains solvent, you can pretty much count on those payments. Companies that default on their bonds face a PR nightmare. Defaults may also cause rates on the company's other debt to rise or possibly force an immediate payment. Given the repercussions, companies only default on their bonds as a last resort. Just like stocks, bonds belong in every portfolio. They diversify and reduce the risk of portfolios containing mostly common stocks. During many periods when stocks spit the bit, bonds perform well. A blend of stocks and bonds should result in a portfolio with lower highs and higher lows than a stock-only portfolio. While bonds can provide capital gains, throughout history, interest has accounted for most bond returns. That lack of capital gains also translates to fewer losses of value—a characteristic that endears bonds to conservative investors. Conservatives and moderates will be drawn to bonds, while aggressive investors may choose to avoid them. Because of bonds' focus on income, they will naturally resonate more with income-seeking investors than with wealth accumulators.

- **Inaccessibility.** Because most discount brokerages don't trade bonds, investors seeking bonds must turn to more expensive sources. In addition, small investors may have trouble creating a portfolio of multiple bonds because the securities tend to sell in $5,000 increments.
- **Research.** While websites like Yahoo! Finance and MSN Money provide a plethora of free information about stocks, you may have to pay for data that will help you analyze bonds.
- **Sensitivity.** Companies issuing bonds have no control over interest rates, yet those rates are the main driver of bond prices. Bond ratings can help investors control for credit risk, but rising interest rates can knock down a bond's price regardless of the issuer's credit quality.
- **Calls.** Some bonds come with call options that allow the bond issuer to buy them back before they mature. If the company calls the bond during a period when interest rates are low, investors who need income may have to reinvest the proceeds from the call at unattractive rates.

Mutual Funds

Mutual funds magnify the purchasing power of investors. They involve an investment company that collects money from a large number of investors and pools it to acquire a selection of securities difficult or impossible for the individuals to own directly. The bulk of mutual-fund assets are invested in stocks and bonds. Within those broad asset classes, managers can pursue a variety of goals. Some funds focus on a particular type of security, sometimes purchasing a large number of companies in an attempt to tap into that segment of the market. If they desire, managers can tighten the focus, such as through buying only small-technology stocks or even limiting themselves to a tiny piece of a sector, such as semiconductors in tech.

Other funds take a broader approach, purchasing a range of investments to capture the benefits of multiple segments of the market. Some funds—known as hybrids—hold both stocks and bonds.

Mutual funds provide investors with the flexibility to pursue any number of complex strategies by purchasing a single security, and they have become immensely popular. According to the Investment Company Institute's "2013 Investment Company Institute Factbook," more than 92 million Americans owned mutual funds in 2012.

Investors purchase mutual funds through brokers, but fund prices don't shift during the day, as happens with individual stocks. Everybody who purchases a fund on a given day pays the same price. ETFs are exceptions.

The first ETF launched in 1993. ETFs operate like mutual funds in that they allow many investors to harness their combined buying power to purchase large amounts of stocks and bonds. However, ETFs differ from traditional funds in a few key ways:

1. As the name implies, these funds trade on exchanges like stocks. That means their prices will ebb and flow throughout the trading day and investors can buy and sell almost immediately.
2. Not all brokers will buy or sell all mutual funds. Many fund issuers prefer to sell directly to investors, and if the issuer makes the process complicated or expensive, some brokers will simply fail to make the funds available. On the other hand, investors can buy ETFs at any time through any broker, without worrying about restrictions posed by the company that created the fund.
3. Because they trade on exchanges, the securities owned by ETFs must be disclosed on a daily basis. Traditional mutual funds can keep their secrets longer.

Most managers of traditional mutual funds attempt to use their skill to outperform the market, or a piece of it. They typically identify an index—a selection of securities designed to track a segment of a stock or bond market—then assemble a portfolio of stocks or bonds comparable to components of the index in hopes of delivering superior returns. This is called active management. Other funds, known as index funds, try to track indexes rather than beat them—a strategy called passive management. Most ETFs are index funds.

ACTIVE VERSUS PASSIVE

Both active and passive strategies have their place, but you should understand the difference between these funds before you make a decision.

Actively managed funds:

- *offer the chance at market-beating returns.* The fact that most managed funds fail to top the market return doesn't change the fact that the upside potential is there.

- *tend to charge more.* Managers expend more time and effort attempting to build a market-beating portfolio than they would in simply matching an index's holdings. As a group, managed funds will assess higher management fees than index funds in the same category. While wise investors won't pay more than needed, the best manager may be worth a higher fee than a lesser rival.

- *allow the manager to freelance.* Just because Morningstar slots a fund into the large-cap value category doesn't mean the fund contains only large-cap value stocks. If you own a managed fund, check the holdings disclosures periodically to see if the manager is still investing in a manner that suits your portfolio.

Passively managed (index) funds:

- *make it easy to target your investments.* Like the prospects for large-cap stocks more than those of others? Then buy a fund that tracks the S&P 500 Index and stop there. You've just bought a piece of the world's most popular index, and your fund will probably deliver a return roughly equal to that of the broad large-cap market.

- *charge lower fees.* Managers make fewer decisions with index funds and the funds make fewer trades, which leads to lower expenses than for actively managed funds. Vanguard is known for charging unusually low management fees for its index funds. When you consider that the object of an index fund is to match the index rather than top it, even a small difference in fees can make one fund look better than another.

- *deliver better performance.* On average, index funds tend to outperform managed funds.

PROS

- **Variety.** According to "Trends in Mutual Fund Investing, May 2014," a monthly report prepared by the Investment Company Institute, 7,848 mutual funds traded at the end of May 2014 plus 1,346 ETFs. These range from broad U.S. stock funds, to foreign-bond funds, to tightly focused sector funds. Whether you seek growth or income, risk or safety, small cap or large cap, you can find a fund that has it.

- **Expertise.** Professional money managers make the decisions regarding buys and sells for mutual funds. When you purchase a fund, you're paying for the managers' experience—often specialized knowledge when it comes to tightly focused funds. Even stock analysts who manage money often rely on bond funds, with the advice of money managers, to fill the fixed-income portion of client portfolios rather than looking for bonds on their own.
- **Diversification (part one).** Regardless of a mutual fund's focus, it will spread its bets by purchasing more than one stock or bond. Investors can overvalue this diversification advantage; a sector fund with 40 tiny biotech companies might deliver more volatile returns than the stock of a large, steady company. As long as you understand the fund's mission and make the right comparison, the diversification argument holds water. If you were planning to purchase one or two individual biotech stocks to gain exposure to that industry, compare your mutual fund to those stocks, then make a decision about which one to purchase.
- **Diversification (part two).** Beyond the diversification of securities within an individual fund, the ownership of the funds itself offers a quick route to a diversified portfolio. Suppose you seek to assemble a broad, blended portfolio of stocks and bonds. Instead of purchasing a variety of stocks and a dozen individual bonds of various maturities, you could buy a large-cap stock fund, a small-cap stock fund, a foreign-stock fund, a corporate-bond fund, and a municipal-bond fund. Maybe those five classes of funds in particular don't work for you, but you could probably find five that would.
- **Reduced time.** Digging into corporate financial statements to analyze individual stocks and bonds takes time and effort. You can research mutual funds much more quickly, in large part because what matters isn't the individual stocks in the fund but the approach and competence of the managers.
- **Lower or no commissions.** Depending on how you purchase a mutual fund, you may or may not pay a commission. However, whatever commission you pay won't come close to what you'd have to lay out to purchase all the stocks or bonds in the fund on your own.

CONS

- **Complacency.** Because fund investors know they're hiring a professional manager to assemble a diversified portfolio, they can easily relax in the knowledge that they've selected a few good funds and forget about the portfolio for a while. Don't fall into that trap. Markets change, industries evolve, fund managers retire, and sometimes portions of the market will stink for a few years. Even fund investors need to keep up with their holdings and make changes at times.
- **Performance.** Fund performance varies widely because of the multitude of investment approaches. In general, funds tend to underperform their benchmarks.

WHO SHOULD BUY FUNDS?

Even more than stocks and bonds, funds fit everyone. Funds allow investors to approximate the returns of just about any portion of the stock or bond market. Wealth accumulation–based to income-based, aggressive to conservative, all styles of investors can find a suitable fund.

Mutual funds appeal to investors in part because they seem safer than individual stocks or bonds. The fund manager purchases a wide range of securities, presumably taking care of the diversification so you don't have to. This assumption doesn't always hold true, but in general a portfolio of 50 stocks will be less volatile than a single stock.

According to a study by *NerdWallet*, only 24 percent of fund managers beat the market over the last decade—and that's not taking into account funds that performed badly enough to disappear during the 10 years ending in December 2012. Active managers outperformed the market by a small margin before fees, but their fees gobbled up all that outperformance.

- **Complexity (part one).** With so many funds available, investors can have trouble determining which ones to purchase. Because mutual funds don't report their holdings in a timely manner, investors have fewer tools for analyzing individual funds for comparison to their peers.

- **Complexity (part two).** Just because you know a mutual fund's name doesn't mean you've chosen which specific part of the fund to buy. For instance, as of May 30, 2014, the AllianceBernstein Value fund came in seven flavors. Each charged different fees, several required different minimum initial purchases, five of the seven were not available to individual investors, and three of the seven levied extra sales charges.

- **Fees.** Every fund deducts expenses. The fund may not advertise that fact and might even hide the fees in the prospectus, but fund managers don't work for free. Those fees bear much of the burden for funds' long-term underperformance. Thousands of funds charge additional fees known as sales loads, nothing more than commissions to compensate whoever convinced you to buy the fund. For example, the AllianceBernstein Value fund Class A shares charge a 4.25 percent fee up-front, which means for every $1,000 you invest, just $955 goes to work for you. In other words, the fund must return 4.7 percent before your holdings return to the value you initially invested. Check your fund's fee structure carefully before investing, and if a fund charges a sales load of any kind, stay away.

If you have trouble imagining a 20% loss in the stock market, you shouldn't be in stocks.

JOHN BOGLE
FOUNDER OF VANGUARD GROUP

6

MOVING TO MAIN STREET

The financial securities on Wall Street appeal to investors because they're made of nothing but money—nothing to store, nothing to guard, nothing to maintain. You check a brokerage statement and get the picture. But for some people, amorphous investments won't cut it. Real estate property has depth that stocks and bonds can't match. Most real estate investors start the same way: by purchasing a house. Houses stand alone in the investment garden, bridging the gap between an investment and a household expense. While stocks and bonds can boost your wealth through price gains and cash payments, houses provide a different kind of return on investment. Yes, homes also tend to rise in price over time. But don't underestimate the value of a home as a place to live. That blend of wealth building and practical usage calls to investors, implanting the lure of real estate into their hearts. Before you dive into real estate, consider a few facts about the asset class:

1. Purchasing a home doesn't prepare you for the rigors of analyzing or managing rental property.
2. Once you purchase anything other than your own home, you in effect take on another job.
3. While you must track your stocks and bonds and keep up with both their prices and the factors that underlie those prices, no financial asset reaches the level of real estate in the time needed to maintain the investment. If those three warnings spooked you, feel free to skip to chapter 7. Real estate investing isn't for everyone. But if you feel the pull to invest in something you can see and touch, consider broadening your investment horizons.

A Real Solid Option

From 1978 through 2013, a 36-year period, the National Council of Real Estate Investment Fiduciaries (NCREIF) Property Index delivered an average annual total return of 9.4 percent. Total returns include both price appreciation and rental income. The index, often used as a proxy for the broad commercial real estate market, contains more than 7,000 commercial properties that combine for a value of more than $300 billion.

While large-company stocks delivered higher average returns during those 35 years, real estate returns came with far less volatility. Standard deviation measures volatility based on the dispersion of returns around the average—the wider the range, the higher the standard deviation. Investors can calculate risk-adjusted returns by dividing the annual return by the annual standard deviation to derive return per unit of risk.

Dividing annual returns by standard deviation yields return per unit of risk. By that measure, real estate trumps both stocks and bonds. The concept may sound complicated, but it does a good job of comparing different asset classes. As the following chart shows, real estate has managed substantially better risk-adjusted returns than stocks or bonds. Real estate prices follow their own trends, and the asset class offers substantial diversification benefits when owned in concert with stocks and bonds.

Commercial real estate values spring from the cash flows the property generates, not its square footage. Analysts calculate bond prices in much the same way, discounting the value of future cash flows. From an investment standpoint, real estate shares some characteristics with both stocks and bonds. However, as a whole, real estate doesn't resemble either of the financial investments.

PROS

- **Upside.** As with stock prices, the value of real estate can keep rising as long as the cash flows continue to expand. There is no upper limit.
- **Dual returns.** Real estate provides the potential for both price appreciation and income. Lease payments provide a bond-like stream of cash flows, while the potential price appreciation should appeal to investors who wish to build wealth.
- **Benefitted by inflation.** Real estate prices and rents tend to rise over time because of inflation. You can augment this growth by improving the property's cash-generating ability. In the long run, real estate prices trend higher, along with prices for just about everything else. Inflation erodes the returns of both stock and bond investors. However, real estate provides a solid hedge against inflation, adding to its diversification value.
- **Proximity.** Unless you live in the middle of nowhere, you can probably invest close to home. Then you can visit the property in person and see what's going on there—sometimes a better option than researching stocks and funds on the Internet.

TABLE 6.1 REAL ESTATE OFFERS HIGH RISK-ADJUSTED RETURNS			
	Returns from 1978 through 2012		
	Property index	Large-company stocks	Long-term corporate bonds
Average annual return	9.4%	12.6%	10.1%
Annual standard deviation	8.0%	16.7%	12.8%
Return per unit of risk	1.17	0.76	0.79

Sources: NCREIF, *Ibbotson SBBI 2013 Classic Yearbook.*

- **Leverage.** You can't borrow money to buy a stock or a bond. But real estate is different. Investors with good credit can sometimes purchase real estate by putting up less than one-third of the price in cash and taking out a mortgage for the rest. The use of leverage magnifies an investor's purchasing power, enabling her to acquire a property otherwise out of her price range. If you put up $50,000 of your own and borrow $150,000 to purchase a $200,000 property, you've upped your stakes. A profit of $10,000 for the year equates to 5 percent of the property value but 20 percent of your investment.

CONS

- **Time.** Real estate doesn't trade on exchanges like stocks, or even over the counter like bonds. Each property must be individually sold to a new buyer, a process that can take a lot of time. When you decide to sell a stock, either because it becomes too pricey or because you worry about its future prospects, the process is as simple as a few clicks on your broker's website. Bond sales require a few more steps, but most of the time you can finish the job quickly. Not so with real estate, which can take months—sometimes years—to sell.
- **Pricing.** As often happens with illiquid markets, prices for real estate can vary from transaction to transaction, even for roughly similar properties. You may have a good idea of your property's worth, but you won't know for sure until you receive a firm offer from a buyer.
- **Learning curve.** You don't know as much about real estate as you think you do. Sure, you've lived in a house or an apartment. You've worked in an office, shopped at a store, slept at a hotel. You may have noticed structural strengths and weaknesses in the buildings, or even considered the characteristics of the building's tenants. While all that means you know something about property, that knowledge won't tell you how to make money from it. Location matters, as does price per square foot. But if you make an investment decision based only on those factors, you might as well use a dartboard.

WHO SHOULD BUY REAL ESTATE?

Based solely on its risk-versus-reward characteristics, real estate should appeal to a broad range of investors. The blend of price appreciation and rental income should appeal to investors from one end of the wealth accumulation/income spectrum to the other. In addition, real estate manages strong returns relative to the volatility of those returns. Such impressive risk-adjusted performance should appeal to both aggressive and conservative investors, not to mention those in the middle.

The choice to invest in real estate involves more than its performance, though. Real estate requires a lot of time to manage. It also demands patience of its owners. People accustomed to selling a stock immediately after making the decision to dump it might have trouble adjusting to the long lead times needed for real estate transactions.

In short, while real estate fits the risk and return requirements for all nine of the investor types presented in chapter 3, individuals not prepared to put some time into their property should probably abstain.

- **People.** A real estate investment is only as strong as its tenants. Sure, all investments can lose value when the business environment changes. However, dealing with people introduces a set of headaches that stock and bond investors don't encounter. Some tenants damage the property, complain all the time, or fail to pay rent in a timely manner. Unless you hire a property manager, you must deal with those troublesome tenants. Of course, if you hire a property manager, you must pay her out of your cash flows, reducing your profits.
- **Leverage.** Yes, leverage is both a pro and a con. While it allows investors to purchase large properties and juice their returns, only a fool forgets about the sharp end of borrowing money. Those interest payments come due every month, regardless of the state of the building. A sour economy could steal your revenue, a tenant could relocate and leave you with empty space, or a fire or flood could force you to shutter some prime cash-generating space. Remember that higher returns generally come with higher risk. Welcome to the world of leverage.

Categories of Real Estate

The pros and cons previously listed apply to real estate as an asset class and to most individual pieces of commercial real estate. That said, different types of real estate have their own characteristics and may require you to modify your approach. Four categories of investment real estate account for more than 95 percent of the market value of the NCREIF Property Index: office, retail, industrial, and multifamily.

Office

Office buildings are the rock stars of commercial real estate. On average they cost more to buy than other properties, and the occasional nine-figure deal captures the investing public's imagination. However, while the skyscrapers that fill America's downtowns are out of most investors' reach, you need not be rich to buy an office property.

The NCREIF says 85 percent of U.S. office buildings and 60 percent of their total market value can be found in the suburbs. Don't write off this less expensive space. Most people who want to invest in office space should begin and end their search in the burbs and focus on class B or class C space, not the ultraexpensive class A. With high rents can come high expenses, and your profits stem from how much cash you have left after covering all the costs. Do your homework, and you can do just fine with class B or class C space.

FIVE THINGS YOU SHOULD KNOW ABOUT OFFICE REAL ESTATE

1. Office space offers excellent growth potential for the 10 years that are coming up. As the U.S. economy continues its decades-long shift toward services and away from the production of goods, demand for offices should remain strong.
2. It is the region more than the neighborhood that is important when scouting locations for office buildings. Look for areas with growing populations, strong economies, and educated workforces. Such regions attract businesses that need office space, and workers will commute to those offices.
3. The average office building in the NCREIF Property Index was worth nearly $60 million in 2010, which may actually be a bit higher due to massive buildings. Nevertheless, if you look around, you can probably find something in your price range.
4. If you want to attract attention, impressive office buildings can do that for you. If you prefer to stay below the radar, consider other types of property first.
5. From year to year, returns on office properties vary more than most. Conservative investors may want to steer clear of them for this reason.

Retail

More than any other type of real estate, the health of a retail building relies on the health of the consumer. Just about all real estate is economically sensitive and could see cash flows decline when times get tough, but retailers often feel the pain first. After all, what do consumers do when they start to worry about the future? Cut back on spending.

Of course, if you are the landlord, you will collect money from retailers via lease payments, so in the near term, a slowdown in consumer spending won't affect your cash flows. However, continued consumer weakness could limit lease renewals and lower the rates you can charge.

Because most retailers rely on a large number of customers coming to the store, you should make sure the retail goals of your tenant fit the area. If a high-end jewelry store leases space in a strip mall known for attracting bargain shoppers, its prospects for renting space might end up being cut short.

FIVE THINGS YOU SHOULD KNOW ABOUT RETAIL REAL ESTATE

1. Retail customers won't travel as far as office workers will, so region is less important than neighborhood.
2. Neighborhoods change over time—often much faster than change occurs in a state or region—and the businesses that rent from you or the people that shop with you will probably change with it. You can't avoid change, and you shouldn't fear it. Just adapt to it.
3. You can find retail buildings everywhere, including in locations not loaded with other retail outlets. If you want to buy close to home, retail may provide more opportunities than office or industrial properties.
4. Large shopping centers account for about half of retail real estate's market value but just 10 percent of the buildings. Investors can find plenty of small, inexpensive properties. At least, inexpensive relative to other types of real estate.
5. You can be successful owning retail real estate without becoming an expert in the retail business. But the more you know about trends in consumer spending and merchandising, the better decisions you'll make.

Industrial

Industrial buildings comprise nearly 20 percent of the market value of the NCREIF Property Index, but they keep the lowest profile. If you want to own property but not generate headlines or get your name in the newspaper, industrial buildings may work for you. Large manufacturing plants attract the most attention, but most of these are owned by the company that uses them and are not for sale—even to the few investors who can afford them.

While the noise and pollution that come with industrial buildings often keep them away from residential and commercial areas, you'll find many of these companies in industrial parks near the edges of cities, in the suburbs, or in exurban areas.

FIVE THINGS YOU SHOULD KNOW ABOUT INDUSTRIAL REAL ESTATE

1. On average, industrial buildings sell for less money per square foot than retail or office properties. However, they also tend to charge less rent, which explains the price differential.
2. The long-term outlook for industrial property is good. Remember, you probably won't buy a factory, but a warehouse or distribution center. In an impatient, information-driven market, many companies have adopted an inventory system

that requires them to house goods in remote areas to limit shipping time, increasing your rental prospects.

3. Because most industrial buildings produce or store goods for shipment else-where, you'll find greater concentrations of them near railroad terminals or ports.

4. Location concerns for industrial buildings involve different issues than those involved with other types of real estate. You don't have to worry as much about proximity to customers as you do about the general condition of the neighbor-hood. Industrial areas often suffer from higher crime rates than other parts of a city or region. If you purchase a building in a rough area, be prepared to pay for a security system, guards, or both.

5. It isn't usually hard to find retail, office, and multifamily properties that are for sale. Not so with industrial properties, which can be located in areas distant from other buildings.

Multifamily

Many beginning real estate investors target apartment complexes because they think they know the industry. In a way, everyone understands residential real estate. Have you lived in a home or apartment? Then you know what tenants expect from these properties. However, understanding the motivations of tenants doesn't always translate to effectively dealing with their problems and demands. More than any other type of real estate, multifamily property is a people business. Apartments tend to be smaller than stores or offices. So if you purchase a 20,000-square-foot multifamily building, you've signed on to service a lot more tenants than would the buyer of a similar-sized building in a different market segment.

FIVE THINGS YOU SHOULD KNOW ABOUT MULTIFAMILY REAL ESTATE

1. Managing residential real estate requires more time than other types of property. Tenants can call 24 hours a day and expect immediate service. If you have a day job or another full-time commitment, expect to hire a property manager to deal with the day-to-day operations of your apartments.

2. Because people always need a place to live, vacancy rates shouldn't rise as high as you might see with office or retail properties during difficult periods—assuming you charge reasonable rents. As a result, your cash flows should remain steadier than most.

3. Another factor contributing to the steady cash flows of multifamily real estate is the large number of tenants in a typical property. When you have three tenants, losing one can turn a profitable business into a loss maker. When you have 30 ten-ants, you can probably absorb it if one or two leave, and find replacements before the next one or two move out.

4. Residential tenants generally lease from year to year, and sometimes month to month, in sharp contrast with the multiyear leases common with other property types. Because of the short-term leases and the larger number of tenants, expect to see a lot of turnover—another reason to hire a property manager who can show apartments during business hours.

5. You may have heard horror stories about the terrible tenant who moves in, doesn't pay, trashes the place, and fights the eviction in court for months. That does happen, albeit not often. Don't let that worst-case scenario frighten you away from multifamily properties, but your awareness of the possibility should drive you to build a cash flow cushion into the investment.

Analyzing and Acquiring Property

After reading the last section, you may have a good idea about what kind of property you wish to buy. It is important to take the time to analyze a property carefully before you purchase it. Be sure to consider the following:

- **Overall cost.** For most investors, a piece of property costs a lot more than the amount they would invest in a single stock, bond, or mutual fund.
- **Concentration.** Few investors should keep more than 25 percent of their portfolios in real estate. That means most investors who aren't wealthy probably won't own more than two properties. Such a focused portfolio puts a premium on getting your selections right.
- **Risk.** While real estate returns offer more return for the risk than stocks and bonds, they expose investors to a different type of risk. Unless you leverage your investment with some sort of derivative securities, you won't lose more on a stock or bond than you put in. Buy $1,000 worth of stock in Rampant Speculation, Inc., and if the company goes under, you're out $1,000. However, real estate isn't just an investment but a business. To maintain real estate, you must cover substantial expenses. If the cash flows suffer, you'll end up covering those costs out of your pocket. If you invest wisely, that shouldn't happen often, but the possibility alone represents a different type of risk.

Remember that even the best investors won't get every investment right. You can best improve your odds by following a thorough, methodical process to ensure you've checked everything you can. If you'd like to invest in real estate, use this seven-step process:

1. **Pick a target real estate category.** Even if you don't have a preference for one type of real estate over another, select a type to look into before you move on to the next step.

2. **Analyze your region.** While you can buy real estate anywhere in the country, if possible, stick close to home on your first foray. If you plan to buy in a large metro area, focus on the city and suburbs. If you don't live near a big city, look at your section of the state. Do some research on the following characteristics:

   - *Demographics.* The more you know about the people who live and work in your area, the better you can assess your needs.
   - *Population growth.* The faster the population grows, the more appealing the real estate market.
   - *Labor.* If you can, focus on areas with low unemployment. The sturdier an area's work force, the more potential tenants will want to locate there.
   - *Construction.* Trends in building permits provide clues about future growth.
   - *Industry.* Spend the time to find out what kind of businesses operate in your target area.
   - *Overall occupancy rates.* Look beyond the occupancy rate of the building you are targeting to that of the broader market in the region.
   - *Rents.* Do the same as you are for the occupancy rates, and look at a broad sample of what people are paying for rent in the area to learn from the trends.

3. **Get specific.** After analyzing the broad market, narrow your focus, identifying a city or neighborhood or key zip codes to target.

4. **Check out the options.** LoopNet and CoStar both claim to be the biggest sources for online commercial property listings. Realtor.com also lists a strong selection in some areas. Narrow down your choices to no more than five prospects.

5. **Pick a team.** Find a broker you trust, preferably someone who focuses on commercial property and has bought and sold investment real estate in your target areas. A broker can probably provide you with plenty of buying ideas as well as occupancy and pricing information. So why wait until this step to get a broker? Because if you let the broker do all the work, you'll come away from the process knowing less than you should about real estate and about the area where you intend to buy. At this point, revisit your favorite prospects, seeking the broker's opinion. She may have some new ideas for you.

6. **Set up your financing.** While both residential and commercial mortgage loans are backed by the purchased property, banks will ask commercial buyers more questions and expect them to possess greater resources and expertise than the typical home buyer. Your broker can help you navigate this process.

7. **Visit your top prospects.** Always, always, always tour the building before you purchase it. You may not be an engineer or a builder or an accountant, but you'll make fewer mistakes buying real property if you get a feel for that property before making an offer.

Two popular ways to value property involve using the capitalization rate and cash-on-cash return. The cap rate reflects operating income as a percent of the property's value. However, property values are both volatile and subjective, and this metric doesn't take into account any leverage.

The cash-on-cash return considers after-tax cash flows divided by the down payment. With real estate, this is as close as an investor can come to the bottom line.

As you tackle steps 4 and 5, you'll want to run some numbers. Your broker can help you assess the properties, but don't make any decisions until you've prepared your own analysis. The Real Estate Worksheet that follows can help. For more info on finding the numbers you need, see the links in the Resources for Researching Property at the end of this book.

Sample Real Estate Worksheet

The worksheet that follows includes the rates for three sample properties: a multi-family brownstone, an office building, and a retail center. The properties are suitable for someone with $500,000 to invest and are calculated with that down payment in mind. The vacancy allowance reflects the average for each property type in the target area.

When you're making your own worksheet, you can get data on asking prices, square footage, rents, and expenses provided by the seller. Expect to make some phone calls (to insurance companies, utilities, etc.) to fill in gaps. A common standard for annual maintenance costs is 1 percent of the property value. It's better to go with 1.5 percent or extrapolate from historical spending if you have the numbers.

Always set aside at least 1 percent of the building's value every year for renovation reserves, more if the property will need extra attention. For example, the professional building in the worksheet needs a new roof and some other upgrades, so it carries a 1.5 percent reserve.

In most cases, you'll fill out your worksheet using some information provided by the seller, some market data you pull from a website or receive from your broker, and some data that you estimate. However, you won't be quite finished.

Just because the former owners of a property charged $15 per square foot doesn't mean you must do the same. Perhaps you can reduce operating expenses to boost profitability. Or maybe you'd rather manage the unit yourself to save money. Here are a few dos and don'ts to consider:

- Explore multiple sources of funding to improve your interest rate.
- Don't change the vacancy allowance, even if you think you can run the building at an above-market occupancy rate. Better to be surprised by the extra money than disappointed because you budgeted badly.

WORKSHEET 6.1 REAL ESTATE WORKSHEET

	Multifamily Brownstone	Professional Building	Strip Mall
Rentable units	10 apartments, each with two bedrooms, 1,200 square feet	Three offices, each 5,000 square feet	Three units, total of 9,000 square feet
Asking price	$1,100,000	$2,000,000	$950,000
Down payment	$500,000	$500,000	$500,000
Loan-to-value	55%	75%	47%
Loan needed (30 years at 6%)	$600,000	$1,500,000	$450,000
Rentable square feet	12,000	15,000	9,000
Rentable units	10	3	3
Annual rent	$18,000 per unit	$17 per square foot	$15 per square foot
ANNUAL INCOME			
Gross potential income	**$180,000**	**$255,000**	**$135,000**
Allowance for vacancy	5%	6%	6%
Real potential income	**$171,000**	**$242,250**	**$128,250**
ANNUAL OPERATING EXPENSES			
Property taxes (available from assessor or seller)	$17,000	$32,500	$14,000
Insurance	$12,000	$9,000	$11,000
Services (trash collection, landscaping, snow removal)	$18,000	$4,000	$4,000
Utilities (gas, electric, water)	$0	$15,000	$11,000
Maintenance	$16,500	$10,000	$14,250
Property management	$0	$7,000	$4,000
Unit for on-site superintendent	$18,000	$0	$0
Operating expenses	**$81,500**	**$77,500**	**$58,250**
Net operating income	**$89,500**	**$164,750**	**$70,000**
Capitalization rate	**8.1%**	**8.2%**	**7.4%**
Renovation reserves	$11,000	$30,000	$9,500
Debt service (mortgage)	$43,168	$107,919	$32,376
Before-tax cash flow	**$35,332**	**$26,831**	**$28,124**
Cash-on-cash return	**7.1%**	**5.4%**	**5.6%**

- Go through the expense section line by line to ensure that you've arranged for the lowest costs. Don't lie to yourself in this area—even aggressive investors should budget conservatively—but also don't just assume the last owner found the best possible price for security services. Maybe you can do better. Perform your own research rather than just assuming you will duplicate the expenses of the prior owner.
- Check the building's rents against the prevailing rate. It may be possible to raise the price.
- Unless you plan to make real estate your business, hire a property manager. Even small buildings with tenants on long-term leases will require some management, with most of the action taking place during business hours. If you can't make the hours and costs work by hiring a property manager, then the deal probably won't work. But if you'd like to try your hand at managing property, do your research before taking the plunge.

An Easy Alternative

Investors who want to get real-estate exposure without the hassle of analyzing, purchasing, and managing physical property can instead turn to the financial markets. Real estate investment trusts (REITs) sell like stocks, though they're technically trust units. Most REITs invest in real estate, though some focus on mortgage loans or a combination of both real property and loans. Some REITs hold diverse property portfolios while others concentrate on certain segments of the market, like retail or office property. These companies can avoid taxation at the corporate level if they distribute most of their cash flows to investors. That explains why just about all REITs pay big dividends.

While REITs are not the same as direct real estate investment, they offer a similar blend of price appreciation and income. In addition, because REITs trade on exchanges, you can buy and sell them at the click of a mouse, avoiding the long lead times for sale of real property. REITs also appeal to investors who don't have a lot of money, because you can buy them without a large down payment, paying for as many individual trust units as you wish.

However, REITs don't offer the full diversification benefit of real property; their returns don't march in step with stocks, but historically REITs haven't deviated from stock returns as much as returns on physical property have. Hence, the reduced diversification. And while REIT investors have in effect hired an expert to manage their property, REITs don't provide the visceral appeal of a building you can see and touch.

A Final Thought

Entire books have been written on the topic of real estate investment, so don't expect to become an expert after reading this section. As you finish this chapter, you should know whether real estate makes sense for you. If it does, study this area in more detail. In part because of the complexity of individual real estate deals and in part because of the magnitude of possible mistakes, this type of investment deserves some additional up-front research. See the Further Reading list at the end of this book for additional resources on the topic.

Investors should remember that excitement and expenses are their enemies. And if they insist on trying to time their participation in equities, they should try to be fearful when others are greedy and greedy only when others are fearful.

WARREN BUFFETT

CHAIRMAN OF BERKSHIRE HATHAWAY, 2004 LETTER TO SHAREHOLDERS

7

ALTERNATIVE ASSETS

Buy stocks and you own a piece of a business. Buy bonds and you've lent money to a company. And investing in a piece of real estate is housing a renter or business that's probably not unlike ourselves. However, the world of investments extends far beyond the best-known options. Most investment classes beyond stocks, bonds, and real estate are lumped together under the innocuous classification of alternative assets. Before digging into the world of alternative assets, you'd better learn a few ground rules:

- Do not assume that all alternative assets will work for you. Be very, very selective, preferably sticking to ones you not only like, but understand.
- Most alternative assets don't trade on exchanges. Some don't really trade beyond casual marketplaces like eBay, and specialized subcultures like collectibles, which often only change hands at flea markets or shows put together by collectors. Even the financial assets may not be easy to buy and sell. This means that investors may not be able to make transactions quickly, and may have trouble establishing a value for the assets even if they can find a buyer. As such, most alternative assets work best for investors with long time horizons.
- While the investment community tends to tar all alternative assets with the "risky" brush, some are downright conservative, actually mitigating risk. Judge each one on its own merits, and don't jump to conclusions.

Many alternative assets defy easy classification. That said, this chapter will divide them into three groups: financial assets, hard assets, and not really investments.

Financial Assets

Alternative financial assets are essentially monetary assets outside the categories already discussed—stocks, bonds, and mutual funds. Beyond those three main categories, there are a number of different financial assets to consider.

Futures Contracts

Futures contracts obligate an investor to buy or sell an asset at a predetermined time in the future. While the contract technically requires the investor to deliver or take possession of the assets, investors usually buy or sell an offsetting contract rather than consummate the physical deal. In other words, if you issue a contract to deliver a load of lumber a year from now, sometime between today and the delivery date, you could purchase an offsetting contract to receive a similar load of lumber on the same date, and the contracts would cancel each other out.

While investors from aggressive to conservative can use futures contracts, these investments don't provide income and would appeal more to wealth accumulators. Investors often use futures contracts to speculate, buying or selling them in the hope that the price of the underlying asset will move in a way that allows them to profit when they offset the contract. On the other hand, investors who own a commodity or plan to purchase it may use futures contracts to hedge their risk. For example, if a soybean farmer fears the price of soybeans will fall, he might sell a futures contract to deliver his soybeans after the harvest, locking in a price he likes in order to hedge against a decline.

FIVE FACTS ABOUT FUTURES

1. Investors can heavily leverage futures contracts, making them potentially more profitable and certainly more risky.
2. Because investors can take both long (buying) and short (selling) positions, these contracts offer lots of flexibility.
3. Futures investors pay small commissions on futures relative to other investments.
4. While futures contracts can protect investors against changes in the price of an asset, they are not a perfect hedge.
5. You can buy futures contracts on both physical and financial assets.

Options

Options provide investors the right, but not the obligation, to buy or sell an asset at a set price (the strike price) during a certain period of time. A call option gives an investor a right to buy, while a put option gives the right to sell. Most of the time, when investors talk about trading options, they mean stock options. Here are two examples of ways to use options:

1. Suzy Speculator thinks the price of Connor Carpet will rise. Rather than pay $5,000 to buy 100 shares at $50 per share, she spends $200 for an option to purchase 100 shares at $55. If the stock rises to $60 before the option expires, she can purchase at $55, then sell at $60, making $500 ($5 per share) on the sale for a $300 profit (after subtracting the price, or premium, of the option). Of course, if Connor shares don't hit the target, the options will probably decline in value. Suzy might sell them, probably for less than the purchase price, or hold them in hopes that Connor jumps up to the strike price at the last minute. If Connor fails to reach the strike price by the time the options expire, they'll expire worthless.
2. Suzy already owns 100 shares of Mitchell Metals, and she fears the price of a share will fall from its current $50. So she pays $150 for an option to sell her 100 shares for $45. If the shares fall below $45, she sells at an above-market price. If instead the shares rise, she has in effect purchased insurance against a decline that didn't happen.

FIVE FACTS ABOUT OPTIONS

1. Like futures, options allow investors incredible leeway to take on or mitigate risk, making them suitable for investors all along the risk spectrum. The most speculative options have technically unlimited risk.
2. Investors can buy or sell multiple options at the same time, allowing them to bet that the price of shares will change over time or that it will remain fairly steady.
3. Options contracts are sold in lots of 100 and quoted at the price of one share. If you buy a call option priced at $0.20, you're paying $200 for the right to buy 100 shares at the strike price.
4. If a stock reaches a price at which the option holder can exercise the option at a profit, it is considered in the money.
5. If you sell an option contract on a stock you don't already own, you are said to be "trading naked." This is because you may end up having to purchase the stock at an inopportune price to satisfy the option. For instance, if you were to sell a call option for shares you don't own at $100 and the stock then rises to $110, you would have to buy the shares at the higher price, then sell them to the option holder for $100 to satisfy the option.

Hedge Funds

Hedge funds operate somewhat like mutual funds in that they allow investors to pool their money and buy assets they couldn't afford on their own. But the resemblance to mutual funds is just skin deep. Managers tend to use unusual, and often risky, strategies. Only sophisticated (read: wealthy) investors can buy hedge funds. These hedge funds are famous for using models that investors with advanced degrees in finance can't understand and reporting returns so difficult to follow as to be nearly theoretical.

Because hedge funds can invest in pretty much anything from stocks to real estate to currencies, their risk profiles vary hugely. Some hedge funds try to multiply the market return or even return the inverse, while others attempt to hedge away market risk. All nine of the investor types laid out in chapter 3 could find a suitable hedge fund, though the reputation of hedge funds may scare away the conservative.

FIVE FACTS ABOUT HEDGE FUNDS

1. Only investors who meet one of the income and net-worth requirements ($200,000 a year in income or $1 million in net worth, excluding primary residence) can invest in hedge funds, which as a group are considered high risk.
2. Hedge funds are less closely regulated than most other investments and frequently use leverage to boost returns; both characteristics contribute to their reputation for risk. The Securities and Exchange Commission is paying more attention to regulating hedge funds than in the past, and the regulation will probably get stiffer with time.
3. As of the end of March 2014, hedge funds managed more than $2.2 trillion in investor assets.
4. In addition to a standard expense ratio, hedge funds often charge a performance fee that gives the manager a cut of any returns above the benchmark.
5. It is frequently required that investors keep their money in the hedge fund for several years.

Venture Capital

Venture capital is money investors provide to fund small businesses that they deem to have strong profit potential. Often, start-ups and small firms can't issue stock or float bonds on their own, so they turn to venture capitalists for help, not only for cash but, in some cases, for management expertise.

Some companies put together venture capital funds that allow investors to get involved in a process that only the wealthiest individuals can tackle on their own. Be aware that venture capital is a risky investment best suited for aggressive investors with patience. Don't expect venture capital funds to generate income for investors.

FIVE FACTS ABOUT VENTURE CAPITAL

1. Most venture capital comes from wealthy individuals and financial institutions. Small investors may have trouble tapping into this asset class.
2. Venture capitalists contribute cash in exchange for an equity stake in the business and often expect to have a say in management decisions.
3. Venture capital funds tend to specialize in one sector or industry. Technology is a favorite in this arena.

4. Individuals or small firms that provide venture capital are sometimes called angel investors.

5. Because venture capitalists receive a piece of the company in exchange for their investment, they are often required to provide more funds than the company could borrow from a bank. This largesse is a main reason many companies seek venture capital funding.

Annuities

Annuities provide investors with a guaranteed income stream, making them a popular retirement investment. Most annuities provide tax protections, so investors can deduct contributions from their income and grow the assets tax free until they start withdrawing the income.

The combination of tax-sheltered growth and guaranteed income provided by annuities appeal to both conservative and income-minded investors. However, compared to other investments, annuities tend to deliver modest returns, making them less attractive to aggressive investors and wealth accumulators.

FIVE FACTS ABOUT ANNUITIES

1. Deferred annuities allow investors to contribute money over time, then withdraw it later in life. Another option for investors is to contribute a lump sum to an immediate annuity, then start drawing an income stream right away. Most annuities guarantee payment of the agreed-upon cash flows for life.

2. With most deferred annuities, investors must pay a penalty if they withdraw the money before the target date.

3. In many cases, an annuity will outlive the beneficiary and payments will go to the investor's spouse until the time of death.

4. While plenty of investment companies provide annuities, life insurance companies in particular are known for them. Not surprisingly, many annuities come with an insurance component, and vice versa.

5. Many annuities tack on extra fees, so investors should review all fees carefully before making any investments.

Hard Assets

If alternative financial assets find something of an analogue in stocks, bonds, and mutual funds, hard assets are like real estate in the sense that they consist of concrete, physical items that are not just numbers on a spreadsheet. There are a number of hard assets that make for intriguing investments for some:

Art and Antiques

Art and antiques only qualify as investments when they are in the hands of experts. The same goes for collectibles. Fads such as the Beanie Baby craze have boosted the appeal of collectibles. However, such products have no steady market and rely mostly on the ability of the owner to convince someone else to buy them.

For many individuals, investing in art, antiques, or collectibles represents an effort to turn a hobby or a personal passion into a money maker. If you can pull it off, fine. But even for people who know the market, such "investments" provide irregular returns at best. Even rare stamps and coins, which might be considered high-end collectibles that fall into their own investment class, aren't as reliable growth vehicles as they seemed to be a generation ago. What does all this mean? Don't count on collectibles to fund your child's college or your own retirement.

FIVE FACTS ABOUT ART, ANTIQUES, AND COLLECTIBLES

1. Because it is harder to find parties interested in purchasing these assets, they can be difficult to sell in a timely manner.
2. Because of the lack of an active market for these assets, their long-term returns are difficult to determine. Collectors tend to estimate higher long-term returns than economists and investment professionals do, and both sides have trouble backing up their projections.
3. Investors who wish to make money with collectibles must be ready to trade when the market heats up, because such markets tend to cool down quickly. Timing matters.
4. A number of art funds have cropped up over the last decade, allowing art enthusiasts to pool their resources to buy and sell artworks. However, the market is too small and too new to assess its long-term potential.
5. While collectibles often sell over the Internet, serious traders do a lot of business at shows where they can meet others with similar interests.

Precious Metals

Precious metals fulfill a unique investment niche. Investors can speculate on changes in the price of gold, silver, platinum, or other metals, or purchase them as something to back them up in the event of an economic or political collapse. Whether the latter option can be considered a reasonable means of protection depends on the investor's level of pessimism, but peace of mind can have tremendous value.

You can purchase precious metals in a number of ways, some of which will sound familiar. Futures and options markets offer a variety of contracts with which investors can put their money behind metals. Investors who prefer to play the metals market by owning pieces of mining companies can turn to stocks and mutual funds. Some ETFs track gold prices but don't actually provide investors with ownership of gold. These securities can also incur higher-than-usual tax liabilities.

The truly conservative—those who purchase precious metals because they worry about a political or financial breakdown—often purchase coins or bars, though such investments require an additional investment for storage and security and may be difficult to sell for a good price.

FIVE FACTS ABOUT PRECIOUS METALS

1. Metals, particularly gold, appeal to investors concerned that stocks or bonds won't deliver a return that can outstrip inflation. Like real estate and other types of real property, precious metals represent a hedge against inflation.
2. During periods of political instability, some investors will convert their wealth into gold or other metals, believing that no matter how the problems play out, this type of asset will still have value.
3. Some precious metals, such as silver and platinum, have industrial uses. As such, their prices fluctuate based not only on the perceived comparative safety of other types of investments (a factor that drives gold prices) but also on economic or industry trends.
4. Precious metals follow much different paths than stocks or bonds. Buying even a small position in metals can reduce the volatility of portfolios otherwise made up of traditional financial assets.
5. Big moves in precious metals, like the 10-year gold run-up that took place from 2001 through 2011, attract a lot of attention and draw momentum investors to metals. However, over long periods of time, metals tend to act like other commodities, underperforming stocks and bonds. According to Kitco Metals, over the last 100 years, gold prices have risen at a rate of about 4 percent a year, lagging stocks and all but the shortest-term bonds.

Not Really Investments

Beyond alternative financial assets and hard assets, there are a handful of other ways to use your money that aren't exactly investments—some being much wiser than others.

Life Insurance

Life insurance is not an investment. Salespeople will tell you otherwise. So will some older people who put a lot of value on the death benefit. Regardless, life insurance is just what the name suggests: insurance to protect your heirs from financial hardship should you die unexpectedly. That death benefit is important, and anyone who has dependents should consider owning life insurance. Just avoid policies that blend an investment with the direct insurance protection.

On the surface, life insurance policies blended with investments sound good. However, the problem with whole life, or variable life, or universal life, or any of those other types of insurance that do something in addition to providing a death benefit, is that insurance companies don't fit the profile for managing the average investor's money.

First, they tend to invest conservatively—too conservatively for most investors' needs. Second, they tend to charge fees higher than most people are comfortable paying for the modest returns they offer. Fortunately for insurance companies, few people ask about the returns of the investment component and then compare those returns to alternatives they could pursue at a lower cost. In most cases, investors are better off buying term insurance—low-premium coverage that provides a fixed death benefit for a preset period of time—and investing the funds they would have used to pay the premium in a higher-cost insurance plan.

FIVE FACTS ABOUT LIFE INSURANCE

1. There are dozens of names for life insurance policies. Universal life, variable life, whole life, permanent life, adjustable life, and many others. Whatever the name, read the fine print and make sure you know what you're buying and how much you're paying for it.
2. Some insurance policies, like credit life or mortgage life, are designed to pay off certain obligations when you die. That sounds like a good idea except that you can often do the job for a lower price (and without multiple policies) by simply purchasing enough term insurance to meet those obligations and providing a generous payout to your dependents.
3. Many insurance companies maintain a cash value that the insured can access if needed. Such withdrawals may be subject to income tax, and they usually lower your death benefit—the purpose of the insurance in the first place. Most investors can purchase insurance and set aside cash on their own at less cost.
4. Married people with children are more likely than single people to need life insurance. Even nonworking spouses should consider insurance, for two reasons. First, the working spouse's costs will go up if she must pay someone else to take care of the home and the children. Second, the survivor's life will change in other ways than living without the spouse, and having money can ease the transition.
5. Many people use life insurance to leave a bequest to a charity, providing the organization with a cash gift they could never afford on their own.

Cars, Boats, Expensive Furniture, and Other High-End Goods

Salespeople may tout lots of items as investments, but don't let yourself think that way. Most hard assets other than real estate and precious metals decline in value over time. Nothing that declines in value is an investment. Period.

You may have heard from a friend or relative that the 1957 Chevy she purchased held its value and outperformed other investments. But her opinion might be skewed, in that she might be underestimating the returns of other types of investments and she might actually be one of the rare and lucky souls who purchased a vintage car whose appeal allowed it to sell it for more than its original cost. Don't count on that happening for you.

If you can afford a high-end set of knives that holds its value, or a classic car, or a leather couch with a 50-year wear guarantee, go ahead and buy it. But you'll make better spending decisions if you reserve the word *investment* for things that tend to rise in value over time and for items you purchase for the purpose of enriching yourself rather than enjoying yourself.

*Far more money has been lost by investors preparing
for corrections, or trying to anticipate corrections,
than has been lost in corrections themselves.*

PETER LYNCH
LEGENDARY INVESTOR AND AUTHOR OF *ONE UP ON WALL STREET*

8

PICKING AN
INVESTMENT PARTNER

Individual investors can't buy and sell financial instruments without the services of a broker—an intermediary who is able to execute trades on exchanges and over-the-counter (OTC) markets. Brokers come in two flavors—full-service brokers and discount brokers—each with its own benefits. In general, the more you pay in commissions, or fees for making trades, the more services the broker performs. Are the additional services worth the extra money? Judge for yourself.

Full-Service Brokers

Full-service brokers offer a variety of services in addition to making trades. Investors are offered personalized advice and research reports on individual securities as well as the broad market. Some of these brokers will help you plan your retirement or advise you on tax matters.

Many full-service brokers charge clients a fee based on a percentage of their assets, much like professional money managers. Such fees average between 1.0 percent and 1.5 percent, which many investors might consider high. If you don't take advantage of the complex services these brokers offer, such a fee makes little sense. If you only use your full-service broker to provide you with research and make trades, expect to pay at least $30 for each trade, and possibly more than $100, depending on the broker and the size of your account.

In an age when anybody with a computer can find a wealth of information on a stock or bond and declare herself an expert, full-service brokers take a lot of heat. Of course, the brokers bring a lot of the complaints on themselves; anyone who would charge an investor $50 to make a simple stock trade when dozens of other firms do it for $5 will make some enemies.

Price aside, full-service brokers make sense for some investors. Here are three factors that might lead you toward a full-service broker:

- **Inexperience.** Not everyone wants to dig into the guts of financial statements to determine whether Able Pharmaceuticals looks like a better option than Baker Pharmaceuticals. If you lack the experience, confidence, or interest needed to research your own investments, it makes sense to consider turning to a full-service broker for help.

- **Variety.** Full-service brokers often make more securities available to their clients. You'll probably have trouble finding bonds, alternative assets, and specialty securities such as commodities or currency futures with a discount broker.

- **Complexity.** Jill, age 30, works as a freelance writer and lives alone. She buys stocks and mutual funds in an effort to build wealth. Simple and direct. Jill's mother, Jane, age 60, hopes to sell her consulting business next year. By age 65, she intends to set up a trust to care for a special-needs child, set up a foundation to fund cancer research, and restructure her assets to lower potential estate taxes. A discount broker can provide Jill with everything she needs, but Jane can't afford to go cheap. She needs a full-service broker who can handle her complicated financial maneuvers.

Discount Brokers

The name says it all. Discount brokers focus on making trades, not providing investment advice, and as such can afford to charge less. It's as simple as you deciding to purchase shares of IBM and the broker making it happen and charging you a smaller fee. Fees range from $20 to as low as $1 for some bare-bones brokerages.

If you want to pay the lowest fees, you can make your trades online. Most discount brokers also offer alternative trading options that you can use when not around your computer, but trading via a telephone or other interface tends to cost more. Some discount brokers provide extra services, such as access to investment research. Not surprisingly, the fees of those discount brokers tend toward the high end of the range.

While everyone appreciates a bargain, you generally get what you pay for. Against that backdrop, here are three reasons why you might lean toward a discount broker:

- **Heavy trading.** The more trades you make, the more thought you should give to commission costs. Suppose you have a $100,000 account and make 10 trades a

SEVEN KEY QUESTIONS

Before you select a broker, Investopedia suggests asking yourself these questions:

1. **"How much will I pay?"** While many investors fixate on the commission, don't let that number alone dictate your decisions. Check out the broker's fee structure. How much do they charge to send you a check from your account, administer an individual retirement arrangement (IRA) account, and make trades over the phone? Brokers may charge higher fees for nonstandard trades such as limit orders or lure you in with low commissions that don't last long. Know what you're paying before you write a check.

2. **"Can I afford the minimum?"** Some companies require $10,000 or more to set up an account, while others require far-smaller minimums.

3. **"Does this broker have a good reputation?"** Dozens of companies provide online brokerage services, and just about all of them can execute trades competently, but not all of them execute other services, such as research and customer service, at the same level. Before your make a decision, research the broker to see what other clients are saying.

4. **"Can the broker's website handle the load?"** Visit the broker's website at various times to gauge its speed. While this test is more important with smaller, lesser-known brokers, everyone has read about high-profile outages at massive websites. Pay particular attention to speeds during peak trading hours in the morning and during the hour before trading ends.

5. **"Does the company offer what I need?"** Every broker can trade stocks and funds. But if you want to move beyond those investments, make sure your broker has access to more specialized investments. Expect to pay more for brokers that provide windows to a broader array of markets.

6. **"How much interest will I earn on my cash?"** Find out how much interest a brokerage pays on the cash balance in your account. In a low-interest-rate financial environment, this question doesn't mean as much, as cash and cash-like investments pay almost nothing. However, in general, some brokerages pay market interest rates on cash, while others pay nothing. Find out your broker's policy before committing funds.

7. **"Will the broker respond?"** Even if you intend to trade online, from time to time you'll have to call the broker, possibly with an emergency. Before you select a broker, try calling customer service a few times, preferably at different hours. If the broker routinely makes you wait on hold for more than 10 minutes, think hard before entrusting the company with your money.

year. If you pay $50 per trade using a full-service broker, commissions will eat up 0.5 percent of your assets, versus making up only 0.1 percent at $10 per trade with a discount broker. If you make 40 trades a year, the high commissions you pay with a full-service broker equate to 2 percent of your assets—too expensive for most investors. At $10 per trade, you're just paying out 0.4 percent of your assets.

- **Involved in nothing but trading.** Even if you don't care much about commission costs because you make few trades, you should avoid paying for services you won't use. If you require a broker simply to execute trades and nothing more, you don't need more than a discount broker.

- **Simple trading.** If you don't plan to buy anything more complicated than stocks or funds, you probably don't need a full-service broker. Full-service brokers' advantage lies in their reach to all parts of the investment market. Depending on the level of analysis you do, you probably should consider a discount broker who provides some research. Just as homebodies don't hire travel agents, stock and fund buyers needn't pay extra for access to the futures market.

Financial Advisers

While they are not actually brokers, financial advisers swim in the same pool. Advisers provide personal service, offering investment ideas, retirement planning, and tax advice, among other services. The expertise of financial advisers varies greatly, and your decision to hire one should spring more from your comfort level with the individual than anything else. Some advisers take a personal interest in your financial welfare.

What separates an adviser from a money manager? An adviser, like a broker, can tell you what to buy and sell, but will leave you to make the trade yourself. The money manager makes the buy and sell decisions for you and does all the work. Only you can determine which of these approaches makes sense to you—or if you want to seek outside help at all.

Factors that might drive you toward a full-service broker—such as having inexperience with investments or complex financial needs—could also steer you toward an adviser or a professional money manager. The average adviser can't match the range of expertise you'll find at a full-service brokerage firm but will probably provide you with more personal service.

PART III

Investment Strategies

I nvestors must focus on the future. The first eight chapters of this book reflect that truth, dealing with the planning process as well as the particular types of investments needed to accomplish those plans. Without some focus on how your situation and needs will change over time, though, your investment efforts are nothing but wasted time. Nevertheless, you can't afford to entirely separate yourself from the present.

Back in Chapter 4, you read about the three types of income—earned income, investment income, and passive income. Until now, this book has focused on the latter two types, which most people achieve only via investing.

The focus on investment and passive income makes sense because most people who hold down jobs can't simply boost their earned income at will to make up for a future shortfall from an investment portfolio. Sometimes you can't reach the goal without boosting the amount you invest. Or maybe you just want to get there sooner.

With those outlooks in mind, it's time to turn away from financial investing for a minute and focus on personal investing.

The four most dangerous words in investing are:

"This time it's different."

SIR JOHN TEMPLETON
MUTUAL-FUND PIONEER WHO FOUNDED TEMPLETON FUNDS

9

STARTING A BUSINESS:
THE SUPPLY SIDE
OF INVESTING

Remember that investing means committing resources in order to earn a return. You can invest cash to achieve a financial return, or you can invest your time. Investments of time can reap both personal and financial returns, beefing up the supply side of your financial models. Starting a small business isn't a financial investment. Instead, consider it a second job.

If the business performs well enough, it can grow into a primary job. However, many—probably most—don't make it that far. In 2012, businesses with no employees averaged about $45,000 in annual revenue, a number certainly skewed higher by a small number of big earners. This number suggests most small businesses don't generate enough revenue to support their operators' families without an additional income source.

Only if a business grows large enough so that the owner can hire someone else to manage it while she focuses on other things will it qualify as a financial investment. But even if the business isn't technically a financial investment, you can still consider it an investment in yourself and your future.

According to the U.S. Census Bureau, nearly 23 million businesses with no payroll operated in America in 2012, generating combined revenue of more than $1 trillion. The six sectors with the most businesses (combining to make up 68 percent of all the businesses) provide services, not goods. See Table 9.1 on page 106.

TABLE 9.1 BUSINESSES WITH NO PAYROLL

Sector	Number of firms	Receipts ($1,000)	Avg. receipts per firm ($1,000)
Total for all sectors	22,735,915	$1,030,932,886	$45
Other services (except public administration)	3,522,878	$88,544,766	$25
Professional, scientific, and technical services	3,212,202	$142,974,538	$45
Real estate, rental, and leasing	2,389,906	$227,427,897	$95
Construction	2,346,798	$127,049,119	$54
Administrative, support, waste management, and remediation services	2,006,177	$42,443,032	$21
Health care and social assistance	1,943,028	$59,887,058	$31
Retail trade	1,905,147	$82,494,176	$43
Arts, entertainment, and recreation	1,236,539	$30,281,203	$24
Transportation and warehousing	1,059,040	$69,902,217	$66
Finance and insurance	720,598	$52,045,924	$72
Educational services	603,455	$8,504,722	$14
Wholesale trade	408,487	$37,187,323	$91
Manufacturing	344,658	$16,164,062	$47
Accommodation and food services	340,770	$15,021,102	$44
Information	327,795	$11,784,901	$36
Agriculture, forestry, fishing, and hunting	240,054	$10,613,759	$44
Mining, quarrying, and oil and gas extraction	109,931	$7,820,264	$71
Utilities	18,452	$786,823	$43

Source: U.S. Census Bureau

Characteristics of Successful Entrepreneurs

Lots of people go into business for themselves. *Inc.* magazine says 600,000 new businesses are founded each year. However, running a business isn't for everyone. The U.S. Small Business Administration (SBA), which offers a wealth of information for anyone considering starting a business, has identified six characteristics common in successful entrepreneurs. She must be:

- **A risk taker.** Most investors in the conservative portion of the risk-tolerance spectrum are likely to have trouble adjusting to the rigors of running a business. Any time you start a business, you must accept the risk that it won't take off as fast as you like. With business ownership comes uncertainty—a trade-off you may not be willing to accept.

- **Independent.** Even if you go into business with a friend or family member, you'll need to make a lot of decisions without outside help. Only the confident and thick-skinned need apply. Why thick-skinned? Because no matter what business you start, you'll have to sell a product or service. And a lot of people won't buy it, even if you do a good job selling it. If you can't handle rejection, don't start a business.

- **Persuasive.** Good ideas far outnumber successful businesses, in part because the idea man can't convince others of its merit. Just about every entrepreneur must double as a pitchman, selling the idea to customers, and perhaps to business partners, suppliers, and bankers as well.

- **Able to negotiate.** This is on the wish list, not the "If you don't have this, you'll fail" list. But many small businesses operate on thin profit margins. The better you can negotiate prices with your customers and suppliers, the more money you'll make.

- **Creative.** No business remains successful for long without adapting. Business owners must be able to think on the fly because competitors will enter their business niche, clients will find substitutes for their product or service, and economic conditions will change in a way that negatively affects the company. Entrepreneurs must be prepared to change with the circumstances. Opportunities will arise. Sometimes you'll discover a new market or come up with a new product or service that complements your existing offerings.

- **Supported by others.** Most successful entrepreneurs won't start walking the tightrope without a net. Don't launch a business unless you have someone—preferably several someones—you can ask for advice. Start with family members or friends who operate thriving businesses or try to find a business mentor.

How to Get Started

This book won't try to help you decide on what type of business to go into. Nobody knows your skill set better than you. However, small businesses work better in some sectors than others, as Table 9.1 illustrates. Of the 22.7 million sole proprietorships operating in the United States in 2012, roughly 90 percent provided services, not goods.

Start by identifying a business you can operate without much help, preferably one in a market you know well. If possible, come up with more than one option, because plenty of ideas that sound good when you first voice them lose their luster when you start writing things down.

SHOULD I START A BUSINESS?

Millions of Americans have built substantial wealth by operating a business. If entrepreneurship fits your personality, give it some thought. But before you take the leap, ask yourself these six questions:

1. **"Can I put in the time?"** Only you know how many hours you can spare to start a business. Don't rush to quit a steady job to start a new company, because sometimes even strong business models fail to produce results. If you already work another job, expect to put in a lot of nights and weekends to get the new business off the ground.

2. **"Do I have the expertise?"** Americans may start 600,000 new businesses a year, but by implication that suggests there are also tens of millions of people who do not make the move and set up their own shop. Consider your skills. Can you provide a service or make a product people need? How much help will you require to do the work? One of the reasons small businesses succeed, particularly in the early years, is that the entrepreneur does much—sometimes all—of the work herself. Paying no salaries allows more of the revenue to flow back to the business owner. Don't even think about starting a business until you identify an area where your knowledge and experience can translate into a revenue-generating company.

3. **"Can my family take it?"** Businesses, even successful ones, can put a strain on relationships. Start-up firms consume time, money, and mental energy. If your spouse and older children aren't behind you, think at least twice before starting a business.

4. **"Do I have the temperament?"** Entrepreneurs tend to think differently than the average salaried worker. Are you the type who won't stop working on a project until it's perfect, no matter how long the job takes? Do you routinely stay late at work even if you don't get paid for it? Do you derive as much pleasure from the kind words of colleagues and superiors as you do from the paycheck? While none of those three characteristics is bad, all could hinder your ability to operate a profitable business. When you do the selling, the producing, the billing, and the accounting, time literally is money. The helpful, loyal, no-job-takes-too-long attitude that makes you a good employee won't serve you well when you're the only one on the clock.

5. **"Do I avoid conflict with other people or businesses when money is involved?"** At some point, a client won't pay you, or she'll argue over her bill. A printer will charge you $500 more than the agreed-upon price for a brochure, gobbling up your profit. Someone whose job you underbid the first time will come back to you for another project and won't like your new, higher bid. Successful entrepreneurs don't enjoy confrontation more than any other people, but if these scenarios make you squirm and might drive you to avoid calling the other party for a week or so, entrepreneurship probably won't work for you.

SHOULD I START A BUSINESS?

6. **"Can I handle the money?"** Many business owners hire accountants to manage their books and file tax returns. If you can afford that, then feel free to do it. But in most cases you will need to prepare your own bids, send your own invoices, and call customers who don't pay. These actions give you an understanding of how your business works that you won't get by burying yourself in projects.

Once you've settled on the business, you've got some work to do. The SBA provides 10 steps to follow when starting a business:

1. **Write a business plan.** Business plans summarize what the business does and how it operates. Analyze the market, and include financial projections. Banks will want to see your business plan before agreeing to loan you money, but the plan has other value as well. Anyone can come up with a good business idea, but it is during the process of writing up the business plan that you will identify weaknesses, and hopefully provide solutions or work-arounds.

2. **Seek training.** Most small businesses are started by subject-matter experts. A carpenter turned contractor, a programmer turned tech consultant, a journalist turned freelance writer. Such people may know their own business, but they don't necessarily know business. The SBA provides plenty of free self-directed training (SBA.gov). SCORE, a nonprofit association dedicated to helping small businesses (Score.org), also provides some training materials online. If you'd rather learn from a live person, your local Chamber of Commerce might be able to point you to free seminars in your community. Many colleges offer entrepreneurship programs, and SCORE can also point you to workshops or webinars and connect you with a business mentor to guide you.

3. **Choose a business location.** This matters most if you plan to produce goods or if you need a shop for customers to visit. However, most small service businesses probably don't need a separate office. If you can work out of your home, do it. You'll save money, and if you keep good records, you can probably deduct some of your home-related expenses on your tax return.

4. **Finance your business.** This is another issue more important to some businesses than others. Many small businesses, particularly service companies, don't require much start-up capital. But if your business requires funding, start looking early. The SBA also provides advice on how to estimate costs, prepare financial statements, and borrow money. The SBA provides financial assistance to some businesses, and most banks make business loans, though you should expect more questions and paperwork than is required for a personal loan.

5. **Select a legal structure.** Options include a sole proprietorship, partnership, limited liability company, corporation, S corporation, nonprofit, or cooperative. Some legal protection, and in some cases tax advantages, are provided for business owners by partnerships, LLCs, and corporate structures. However, all of these structures will require time and money to set up and maintain. Sole proprietorships, the most common structure used by start-up businesses, are simple and cheap. You just report your business earnings using the Schedule C on the traditional Form 1040. Sole proprietors maintain control of the business, a big plus for most entrepreneurs. Of course, with that control comes responsibility; just as you can claim credit for success, you'll take the blame for failure. The biggest weakness of a sole proprietorship is that you gain no legal separation between yourself and your business, which leaves you personally responsible for the business's debts and other obligations. Visit SBA.gov to compare the different business structures.

6. **Register the business name.** Do this through your state government.

7. **Get a tax identification number.** This instruction doesn't apply to all businesses. According to the IRS, your business needs a federal employer identification number (EIN) if it meets any of the following criteria:

   a. It has employees.

   b. It operates as corporation or partnership.

   c. It files employment, excise, or alcohol, tobacco, and firearms tax returns.

   d. It withholds taxes on income other than wages paid to a nonresident alien.

   e. It maintains a Keogh retirement plan.

   f. It is involved with certain types of trusts, estates, mortgage investment conduits, nonprofit organizations, farmers' cooperatives, or plan administrators.

   g. Most small businesses don't need an EIN, though if you expect to have employees in the next year or so, you might as well apply for one. Talk to your state to determine whether you need a state tax ID number.

8. **Register for state and local taxes.** Each state and municipality has its own tax laws. Research those before you start marketing, and certainly before you start billing, to ensure that you comply with the laws. SBA.gov provides links for each state, or you could just visit the websites for your state and municipality. Pay particular attention to sales tax requirements. They vary from state to state; even within a given state, not all businesses may face the same requirements.

9. **Obtain business licenses and permits.** Most businesses won't need these. However, you should play it safe by checking whether you need federal, state, or local permits. The SBA can also help you with this.

10. **Understand employer responsibilities.** At first blush, this one sounds like government-speak warning entrepreneurs to be good bosses. But the SBA has something specific in mind. Here is a list of steps to take before you hire your first employees:

a.   Obtain an employer identification number (EIN).
b.   Set up records for tax withholding.
c.   Verify employees' eligibility to work.
d.   Report new hires to the state.
e.   Obtain workers' compensation insurance.
f.   Post required notices in the workplace—not as much of an issue if your employees work off-site.
g.   File your taxes. Most employers must file Form 941 quarterly to report how much they've withheld from employees' wages.
h.   Get organized and stay informed. This is some of that government-speak mentioned earlier, but it makes sense. Once you hire an employee, you rise to a higher profile with taxing authorities and make yourself more of a target for legal attacks. Pay attention to the law and changes in the law while working to maintain a fair workplace. Happy employees are less likely to sue the boss.

If you think starting a business sounds like a lot of work, you're right. Remember, a small business isn't an investment, but a job. Although you may find the job rewarding, never lose sight of the fact that most small businesses generate revenue for their owners because the owner does a large part of the work, or at least directs the work.

You can save some time by purchasing an existing business, in effect buying the convenience of not having to establish a customer base. When you buy a business, you can review the books to make sure it's in good shape. And review the tax returns, records, customer rolls, and other documents.

If you have the money to purchase a preexisting business that provides a revenue stream for an owner who doesn't have to work for the company, good for you. Invest that stream of passive income in securities that will rise in value. However, most individuals will find such businesses too expensive to buy.

Businesses you operate yourself tend to cost less than those providing passive income, and many investors will be able to afford only the former. Of course, that limits your options to businesses you understand. As a rule of thumb, if you expect to actually work at the business you purchase, stick to an industry you know well enough to launch your own start-up.

The purchase of a small business generally entails less risk than starting a similar business on your own. Just as with financial investments, you're paying a premium for that security in the form of an up-front purchase price. However, buying a business won't work for everyone.

Remember that 90 percent of one-person businesses provide services, and many service businesses are driven by the owners' relationships with her clients. Don't expect to purchase a consulting business and retain clients who patronized the business because they trusted the founder.

SO YOU WANT TO BUY A BUSINESS?

Regardless of whether you buy from an acquaintance or a stranger, do your research before writing a check and don't believe everything you read. When analyzing a business for purchase, consider these factors:

- **Previous owner's income.** You want to see what the seller pockets after paying suppliers, employees, expenses, taxes, and any other costs. Look at the total amount the owner brings in, then check the trends to see if it's growing, or at least steady. If the seller tells you the books understate her personal profits because she sometimes draws money directly from the business, consider whether someone trying to cheat on her taxes wouldn't hesitate to cheat you as well. Spend some time checking out the business's accounts or debts receivable—money owed to it by customers or firms it works with. Don't let the owner dazzle you with promises of cash flows that won't materialize.

- **Business environment.** Analyze the business's key market. Employment and housing trends will tell you whether potential customers have money to spend. Demographic analysis will tell you whether the population is trending older or younger, richer or poorer—key information for a business owner. Remember, you can't just buy a business and sell it in six weeks like a stock. You need to be confident the region will continue to support your business for the next few years or longer.

- **Tax liabilities.** Don't get stuck with the former owner's sales tax liabilities. If the business is required to charge sales tax, ensure the seller is up to date before buying.

- **Reputation.** This will take more work if you purchase a business in a community where you don't live. If the business has a bad reputation—deserved or undeserved—you could be buying a headache. Check newspaper stories about the business and look for profiles online. Talk to locals if you can, prowling popular hangouts to test the temper of the community. This takes time, but if you learn the former owner has a reputation that caused community groups to boycott her store, you'll be glad you checked it out.

- **Competition.** No business operates in a vacuum. Find out which companies are the biggest rivals of the firm you wish to buy. If the owner won't tell you, consider her reticence a yellow flag and do your own research. Have new businesses jumped into the fray, carving the pie into smaller pieces? Has the target market changed? Are new products or services rendering your target business obsolete? The more you know, the better your chances to argue the price down or avoid the deal altogether.

Business owners often sell to people they know, bypassing a public sale. If you can buy in that way, more power to you. Alternatively, you can seek out a business broker or visit a website like BizBuySell.com, which claims to have 45,000 active listings and more than 100,000 successful sales of businesses. An Internet search could also provide other business marketplaces.

One type of business popular with investors is a franchise. Many businesses—most notably fast-food restaurants—grant licenses allowing operators to run a business using the parent company's name. Franchises have appeal because the buyer can tap into the power of a larger company's brand and in some cases its marketing efforts. Franchisees generally pay the parent company up-front and then pay periodic licensing fees or a percentage of revenue.

More than with other businesses, franchises often come complete with a location, management training, and a staff to operate the business. Some franchisees purchase the business, then hire a manager to run it and try to create a passive income stream. Depending on how well the business performs, this may or may not work. Plenty of franchisees jump in and choose to operate the business themselves, potentially fattening up the bottom line.

Franchises offer several benefits not usually found with other types of business purchases:

- Brand-name recognition and the commensurate built-in customer base
- A proven business model that has presumably worked in other areas. Companies that sell franchises generally provide buyers with a blueprint for operating the business, limiting the buyer's chance of making mistakes.
- Either an existing location with a recognizable name or assistance setting up a business in your area

While franchises offer buyers a chance for independent operation, the freedom isn't complete. Buyers must follow detailed franchise agreements and in many cases have little recourse if they get into a dispute with the parent company. Many a franchise deal has fallen apart because the buyer didn't like the restrictions about products, pricing, or management policies laid down by the company selling the franchise. Other disadvantages of franchises include:

- **High costs.** You'd expect to pay more for an established business and brand. But in addition to potentially high up-front costs and fees for licensing or revenue sharing, the franchisor might bill the franchisee for a share of national or regional advertising costs or require the purchase of supplies at higher prices than the business could find on its own.

- **Reputation risk connected with the parent company.** Just as you purchase access to a powerful brand, you also buy any problems or scandals connected to that brand. Remember the disastrous Exxon Valdez tanker spill in 1989? Nearly 11 million gallons of oil flowed into Prince William Sound in Alaska, and the backlash crimped sales at Exxon stations all over the country, many of them operated by franchisees that had nothing to do with the company's oil operations.
- **Franchises are rarely permanent.** If the parent company decides to rescind the license, a franchisee may have no way to contest the move.

No matter what kind of business you're looking at buying, assign it a value based on the income it provides and, to a lesser extent, on the value of property or inventory it owns. Business-valuation analysis is complex, and most investors should hire an experienced accountant or consultant to help them with the process. If you'd like to make a go of it yourself, SCORE (Score.org) offers a worksheet that can help you assign a value to a business.

But don't live or die by the spreadsheet, as not all businesses trade at the same multiple of earnings. However, the sheet can provide you with a ballpark figure and allow you to compare the company's price with the value of other similar businesses to determine whether the asking price is too high. Remember how any investment, no matter how attractive, can rise to a value at which it's overpriced? The same goes with businesses, but the money at risk in a business purchase probably dwarfs what you'll shell out for a single stock or bond.

The bottom line is that if you're not confident you'll get a good deal, don't buy the business. Walk away from the deal and find another one.

The true investor scarcely ever is forced to sell his shares,

and at all other times he is free to disregard the current

price quotation.... Thus the investor who permits himself

to be stampeded or unduly worried by unjustified market

declines in his holdings is perversely transforming his basic

advantage into a basic disadvantage.

BENJAMIN GRAHAM
THE INTELLIGENT INVESTOR

10

DIVERSIFY YOUR HOLDINGS

Most investors don't think much about diversification until they notice all of their stocks falling through the floor during a market downturn. Wise investors don't wait to diversify until it's too late.

Why Diversify?

If you buy nothing but stocks, you'll go to bed with a smile during bull markets and pull your hair out during bear markets. Diversification can protect you from the worst of the downs, at the cost of missing out on some of the best of the ups.

Not surprisingly, the closer you come to needing the cash, the more important diversification seems. Nobody likes to see her portfolio decline in value, but it would feel worse if it happened three years before her daughter started college. Diversification makes sense even during strong markets, and even for investors with a long time horizon, for at least three reasons:

1. **Life doesn't always go as planned.** A medical emergency, job loss, or lawsuit could put pressure on your retirement savings long before retirement.
2. **Volatility makes a lot of investors nervous.** Diversification reduces volatility, which means investors rest easier.
3. **You never know which asset class is going to take the lead over the next year.** Yes, stocks tend to outperform bonds over long periods of time, but bonds have plenty of good years, sometimes coinciding with weakness in stocks.

TABLE 10.1 BLENDING STOCKS AND BONDS			
Portfolio	Annual return	Standard deviation	Return per unit of risk
100% large-company stocks	11.8%	20.2%	0.58
90% stocks/10% bonds	11.2%	18.2%	0.62
70% stocks/30% bonds	10.0%	14.5%	0.69
50% stocks/50% bonds	8.9%	11.3%	0.79
30% stocks/70% bonds	7.8%	9.2%	0.85
10% stocks/90% bonds	6.7%	9.0%	0.74
100% long-term government bonds	6.1%	9.7%	0.63

Sources: *Ibbotson SBBI 2013 Classic Yearbook*, Morningstar.

For an example of the power of diversification, consider Table 10.1, which considers portfolios with only two types of assets: large-company stocks and long-term government bonds.

The returns in Table 10.1 assume investors purchased their portfolios at the start of 1926, then rebalanced to the original weighting at the end of every year through 2012. Return per unit of risk measures the balance between risk and reward. The portfolio with 30 percent stocks and 70 percent bonds offers the most return per unit of risk, but investors who seek more reward or less risk may prefer to deviate from that ideal.

Not surprisingly, the 100 percent stock portfolio outperformed the 100 percent bond portfolio, and every incremental addition of stocks boosted the return. This makes intuitive sense, just like every spoonful of sugar you add to a cup of coffee makes it sweeter. Only your personal taste dictates how much is too much.

However, returns don't tell the whole story. Standard deviation measures how widely a portfolio's returns deviate from the average return. For example, the chart suggests that portfolios containing 50 percent stocks and 50 percent bonds averaged an annual return of 8.9 percent with a standard deviation of 11.3 percent. Those numbers imply that the 50/50 portfolio managed a return within 11.3 percent of 8.9 percent (for a range of –2.4 percent to 20.2 percent) in two-thirds of the years tested.

As the percentage of stocks in the portfolio rises, so does the standard deviation, the most common proxy for risk. The chart also presents the return divided by the standard deviation, labeled as return per unit of risk.

Based on these numbers, a portfolio of 30 percent stocks and 70 percent bonds offers the best ratio of risk to return. Of course, if you require a return greater than 7.8 percent, you'll need more stocks than 30 percent. Don't forget to correct for inflation, which has averaged 3 percent a year over the long haul.

Every aspect of constructing an investment portfolio revolves around trade-offs. Accept greater risk and receive greater return and so on. The more dissimilar types of assets you add to a portfolio, the more diversified that portfolio. Of course, you can overdiversify by purchasing a little of everything. Even the shrewdest investors with loads of time to spend analyzing securities can run into trouble this way. Most investors—particularly individual investors—shouldn't need more than five types of assets in a portfolio:

- Large-company stocks, including stock-oriented mutual funds or ETFs
- Small-company stocks, including stock-oriented mutual funds or ETFs. These tend to be more volatile than large-company stocks but provide higher returns.
- Bonds, including bond-oriented mutual funds or ETFs
- Real estate, in the form of real estate investment trusts (REITs)
- Alternative assets—not the hedges but the investments designed to bet on price movements to generate high returns at substantial risk

Of course, you need not own all five. In fact, millions of investors will never purchase real estate beyond an owner-occupied home and will avoid alternative assets of all types. In addition, there are many more types of assets you might choose to select, most notably foreign stocks and a diversified list of bonds.

For the purposes of this example, however, five types of assets are plenty. These assets offer varied levels of diversification relative to each other. Some types of bonds—high-yield (junk) or convertible bonds—offer less diversification for a stock portfolio than traditional bonds. Real estate offers solid diversification benefits for both stock and bond portfolios, but investors who gain real estate exposure through REITs will find that those securities are more highly correlated to stocks now than they were years ago.

Not all asset classes provide the same type of diversification relative to other assets. Table 10.2 estimates the diversification effect of assets relative to other assets. Within these broad ranges, subsets of each asset class will have different diversification characteristics.

Correlation reflects how closely securities move together. Assets with exact correlation move in lockstep, while those with exact negative correlation move in precisely opposite directions. Most assets have correlations somewhere in the middle.

Alternative assets as a whole offer substantial diversification benefits for most asset classes but not all. You'd expect venture capital, which is invested in the equity of start-up companies, to be more highly correlated to stocks (also equity investments) than to bonds.

Realize that diversification is not an exact science. Given the illiquid nature of many markets, even measuring the volatility of historical portfolio returns can be difficult, which suggests that estimating future volatility is even tougher.

TABLE 10.2 DIVERSIFICATION BENEFITS				
	Large-company stocks	Small-company stocks	Bonds	Real estate investment trusts
Alternative assets	Substantial	Substantial	Substantial	Varies
Real estate investment trusts	Moderate	Low	Substantial	–
Bonds	Substantial	Substantial	–	–
Small-company stocks	Low	–	–	–

Portfolio construction relies on more than just an understanding of asset correlation. Each investor's idiosyncrasies must also be taken into account, which explains why you can't simply plug some numbers into a spreadsheet and spit out the perfect portfolio. Two investors with the same approach to investing may require different portfolios because of their age, wealth, or financial goals.

One popular strategy for allocating assets is to subtract the investor's age from 110 and use the remainder as the percentage of her assets to put in stocks, placing the rest in bonds. Using this equation, a 30-year-old will have 80 percent in stocks and 20 percent in bonds, while a 70-year-old would have 40 percent in stocks and 60 percent in bonds. However, like so many financial equations, this allocation tool is just another rule of thumb because so many factors besides age make a difference. Plus, many investors want to own more than just stocks and bonds.

All else equal, the following factors should skew investors toward taking on more risk:

- High wealth
- Young age
- Good health
- Long time horizon
- High tolerance for risk
- Goals that require high investment returns

Of course, investors who don't fit this profile—those who are older or less wealthy or whatever the circumstance may be—should skew toward less risky portfolios.

Fortunately, you need not follow an exact formula to effectively diversify your portfolio. Even experienced portfolio managers with similar investment approaches might construct drastically different portfolios for the same client. Sometimes you

	Base portfolio (moderate approach)	Aggressive approach	Conservative approach
Large-company stocks	30%	30%	25%
Small-company stocks	5%	15%	0%
Bonds	55%	40%	65%
REITs	10%	5%	10%
Alternative assets	0%	10%	0%

TABLE 10.3 ABIGAIL ABBOTT PORTFOLIO

can create multiple portfolios of similar risk using widely different collections of assets. The following portfolios should help you make your own investment decisions. Don't use the asset allocations as gospel, but pay attention to how the base portfolios for each of the three hypothetical investors differ and how those portfolios change based on investing style.

Portfolio 1: Abigail Abbott

Abigail, age 65 and single, just retired after more than 40 years as a legal secretary. She's saved up enough to fund a modest lifestyle but worries that she will outlive her money.

- *Wealth*: moderate
- *Age*: retirement
- *Health*: good
- *Time horizon*: already living on investments
- *Goals*: moderate, tempered by concern about outliving investments
- *Focus*: income

Subtract Abigail's age from 110, and you get a target 45 percent stock allocation with 55 percent in bonds. Given Abigail's modest lifestyle and moderate goals, she doesn't need to be aggressive. But at the same time, given her concern about outliving her income, she can't simply ignore high-return investments such as stocks.

Now suppose Abigail takes an aggressive approach to investing, implying a higher risk tolerance and a strong desire for higher returns. Abigail trades in some of the bonds and REITs in favor of small-cap stocks and a 10 percent allocation to risky alternative assets. If, on the other hand, Abigail chooses to play it conservatively, her portfolio might end up with more bonds, a lower stock allocation, and no alternative assets.

TABLE 10.4 BARRY BARRYMORE PORTFOLIO			
	Base portfolio (moderate approach)	Aggressive approach	Conservative approach
Large-company stocks	40%	40%	45%
Small-company stocks	30%	55%	15%
Bonds	25%	10%	40%
REITs	0%	0%	0%
Alternative assets	5%	15%	0%

Portfolio 2: Barry Barrymore

Barry, age 35, just got promoted to manage his advertising agency's West Coast office. He's married with two kids, ages five and two. Barry brings home a big paycheck and spends money on a big lifestyle. He's invested 15 percent of his income since his first job out of college and hopes to retire at 55, when his youngest son graduates from college.

- *Wealth*: high
- *Age*: prime earning years
- *Health*: good
- *Time horizon*: kids have 13 years until college, Barry has 20 years until retirement
- *Goals*: aggressive targets, but manageable given his income
- *Focus*: wealth building

Barry has already stashed away a generous portfolio, and he can afford to invest for the long term and absorb plenty of risk. However, while Barry has set high goals for his portfolio, given his future earnings power he doesn't need to take on excess risk to meet them.

Subtract Barry's age from 110 and you get a 75 percent stock allocation and 25 percent in bonds. The bond allocation makes sense for diversification purposes, leaving 75 percent to divide among riskier assets (40 percent in large-company stocks, 30 percent in small-company stocks, and 5 percent in alternative assets).

If Barry were to take a more aggressive investment approach, he might dip to 10 percent bonds and move his assets into small-company stocks (raising them to 35 percent from 30 percent of his portfolio) and alternative assets (increasing them to 15 percent from 5 percent). From the conservative perspective, Barry knows he doesn't need 75 percent in risky investments to meet his goals. He puts 40 percent in bonds and the rest in stocks, with three-fourths of the stock allocation in large companies.

TABLE 10.5 CLIFF CLEVINGER PORTFOLIO			
	Base portfolio (moderate approach)	Aggressive approach	Conservative approach
Large-company stocks	60%	45%	45%
Small-company stocks	30%	40%	15%
Bonds	10%	0%	25%
REITs	0%	0%	15%
Alternative assets	0%	15%	0%

Portfolio 3: Cliff Clevinger

Cliff, age 20 and single, drives a forklift at a textile warehouse. He doesn't make much now but hopes to eventually work his way into management. Cliff doesn't know much about investing but participates in his company's tax-deferred retirement plan. He'd like to marry, have kids, and buy a house, but is in no hurry.

- *Wealth*: low
- *Age*: young
- *Health*: excellent
- *Time horizon*: more than 40 years to retirement
- *Goals*: uncertain in both time and scope
- *Focus*: wealth building

Based on Cliff's age, the stock/bond allocation equation suggests he should hold 90 percent in stocks and 10 percent in bonds, an allocation that makes sense for him because he requires no income from his portfolio.

While Cliff can afford to invest aggressively, he decides to avoid complicated investments until he learns more about them. He ends up putting 90 percent in stocks, using a simple model, placing 60 percent in large-company stocks and 30 percent in riskier small stocks.

If Cliff takes an aggressive bent, he might look into alternative assets (making them 15 percent of his portfolio) and boost his small-company stock exposure to 40 percent from 30 percent. At 20 years old, he really doesn't need bonds.

Even if he decides to go with a conservative angle, Cliff shouldn't place more than 25 percent of his money in bonds. He has too much time ahead of him to absorb short-term losses and benefit from compounding. With this thinking, Cliff reduces his alternative assets and lowers his exposure to risky small-company stocks in favor of REITs, which he purchases for diversification purposes, not for income.

Your Own Portfolio

When building your own portfolio, blend what you know about investments with what you know about yourself, with the goal of reaching your personal financial objectives—not your parents' objectives, or those of your friends, or of your boss, or your professor. Spend as much time as it takes to determine the proper asset allocation—the percentages you will devote to each asset class—for your portfolio. Vanguard's Investment Counseling & Research group estimates that asset allocation can account for about 90 percent of portfolio performance.

Does this mean you shouldn't attempt to select superior stocks, bonds, and mutual funds? Not at all. But, according to Vanguard, if you emphasize the wrong asset class and craft a portfolio that is too aggressive or conservative for your situation, you'll have to find a lot of big winners to make up for it.

Investing should be more like watching paint dry

or watching grass grow. If you want excitement,

take $800 and go to Las Vegas.

PAUL SAMUELSON
THE FIRST AMERICAN TO WIN THE NOBEL PRIZE FOR ECONOMICS

11

TRACK YOUR PROGRESS

Before a boxing match, reporters once asked Mike Tyson how he would deal with his opponent's plan to move laterally and dance around in an effort to keep the heavyweight champion from landing the big punch. Tyson responded, "Everybody has a plan until they get punched in the mouth."

Tyson's verbal retort should connect with every investor, because he makes a good point. Your plan looks good now, but at some point you'll encounter a situation you didn't expect, and the plan's weakness will be exposed.

Don't take it personally; every plan has a weakness. As a diligent investor pursuing goals in real life and not just on paper, you will want to make a point of reviewing your plan and keeping an open mind about changes. Be careful with this one. But while you can't just crank up your long-term plan and forget about it, trusting it to reach its target without assistance like a cruise missile, you also don't want to revisit it too often—particularly if you have a tendency to worry or tinker.

Worriers should go against their instincts and spend less time watching their investments than the average investor. That goes double with the long-term plan. If you've created models to fund costs 10 or 20 years in the future, you gain nothing by sweating over them week to week, or even month to month. No matter how bad a month is, you shouldn't decide whether you need to change your asset allocation based only on that month.

While everyone's situation is different, you should keep the following considerations at the forefront of your mind when maintaining your plans.

Keeping Track of Individual Investments

Review your individual investments at least twice a week. If you're the type to worry a lot about short-term market movements, don't check your portfolios every day. You might miss some news, but you might also keep your blood pressure manageable.

Investors who aren't particularly risk averse should check their stocks and mutual funds every day. Don't worry so much about the prices, as stocks and stock funds in particular can be quite volatile on a day-to-day basis. Check them if you like, but don't knock yourself out to do it every day, and certainly don't worry much about one- or two-day movements.

News is another story. Review the headlines about your investments as often as you can. Fortunately, the Internet makes this process easy. For a simple way to track your investments, input the stocks, mutual funds, and any other exchange-traded investments in a portfolio at one of these three websites: Finance.yahoo.com, Money.msn .com, or Google.com/finance. Each of these sites allows you to track your portfolio's performance and read the latest news stories that mention the companies you invest in. They also provide links to statistics and other tools for researching investments.

Knowing When *Not* to Sell

When an investment's price changes drastically and the news suggests something has changed, it's time to consider whether to sell the stock. The research performed on this topic could fill a small library, and the sell decision is as personal as it gets. While only you can make the final call, here are five reasons *not* to sell:

1. **Your investment has declined in value along with the broader market.** If your stock is down 15 percent over the course of three months and its benchmark—using, for example, the S&P 500 Index of large-company stocks or the Russell 2000 Index of small-company stocks—has fallen a similar amount, don't panic. Remember that corrections, or broad declines in the market, are a part of investing. No investment increases every day. The goal is to find securities that manage enough positive days to offset the negative days and, hopefully, beat their benchmark. If you own a diversified portfolio of high-quality investments that seem capable of reaching your investment targets over time, ride out the market's weakness and don't try to time the declines. You won't be able to identify the market's bottom or top, so don't try. Even professionals who attempt to do this are usually wrong.

2. **Your brother-in-law or a colleague tells you a company is a terrible investment.** Perhaps it is, but just like you shouldn't buy simply because someone says this stock will go through the roof, don't be quick to sell on similarly tenuous suggestions. If you trust the person who advised you to sell, research the company and make your own decision.

3. **The financial media reports bad news.** Sometimes you need to sell on bad news. But companies generating hundreds of millions of dollars a year in revenue will often—and, in fact, usually do—end up shaking off bad news. A lawsuit or a product recall or a scandal involving an executive will make headlines, and, in some cases, will cause your securities to dip in price. However, unless the bad news is likely to affect a company's revenue and profits, don't use the stories to justify a sell decision. Review each situation individually.

4. **Other people are selling.** Investors sell stocks, bonds, and mutual funds every day for a variety of reasons. Don't overvalue the news that some of your friends, or even company executives, are selling stock. Of course, you should try to find out why they're selling. If friends are bailing out, talk to them. If major investors or executives are selling, you might find news stories about the sales. But only after you assess the rationale for the sales should you decide whether to follow the trend.

5. **The investment has performed very well.** It is often thought that once a security becomes way too expensive, you should consider bailing out. Yes, research shows that stocks with low valuations—stocks that trade at a lower-than-average multiple of their earnings, sales, or cash flows—tend to outperform more expensive stocks. Thus, if your investment looks too expensive, don't be afraid to sell it. But when a security rises because of good news, it's doing what you purchased it to do. Decades of academic and industry research has shown that stocks that rise in price tend to continue rising. This isn't an absolute, but the trend is strong enough to suggest that it's foolish to sell just because your stock is on the rise.

Knowing When to Sell

All of this begs the question, "When *should* I sell an investment?" The simplest answer is that you should sell it when the reason you purchased it is no longer valid. In other words, if you purchased a stock because it looked cheap, consider a sale after the shares rise to the point that they look expensive. If you purchased a bond because the issuing company had a strong credit rating, consider a sale if that rating deteriorates.

Here are five factors that should lead you to consider selling an investment:

1. **Weakening fundamentals.** This applies more to stocks than other investments. If you purchased a stock because of its growth rate, profitability, valuation, or strong balance sheet—or a combination of these factors and others—it may be time to sell when the company looks less attractive on these metrics.

2. **Changing environment.** With stocks, possible game changers include new products that render your company's offerings obsolete or government regulations that make it more difficult for your company to make money. Interest-rate changes can have a huge effect on bonds, but if you purchased them for the income they provide and don't believe the company will default on its debt, selling bonds

at a loss for any reason other than a major change in the issuer's creditworthiness rarely makes sense.

3. **Merger taking place.** If your company accepts a purchase offer, you may enjoy a big leap upward in price. Check your stock's current price and compare it to the price the acquirer plans to pay. Most stocks trade at a discount to the final bid price to reflect the possibility that the merger won't go through. You can hold onto the stock in hopes of collecting the full merger price or because you think the acquiring company is a good investment and don't mind your stock being connected to that company's stock. Some mergers are funded with cash, some with stock, and many with a combination. Regardless of the deal terms, always revisit a stock and consider a sale after a merger offer.

4. **Something better comes along.** This applies mostly to investors who develop an expertise at selecting securities and do their own analysis. Just because the guy who gave you the tip to buy Cogswell Cogs last month now wants you to dump Cogswell and buy Spacely Sprockets doesn't mean you've found something better. However, if after careful analysis, you think Spacely offers a lot more upside than Cogswell and you don't want to own both, then sell Cogswell and buy Spacely.

5. **Sleepless nights.** No investment is worth keeping if it robs you of peace. Remember the earlier advice not to sell simply because of bad news? That still applies, unless the news keeps piling up and has you dreading the daily portfolio check. Don't use this last reason as a justification to sell a bunch of securities. It only applies to those that worry you to the point that they affect your well-being.

Knowing Your Long-Term Goals

Just as you only sell an investment when the reasons you purchased it no longer apply, you shouldn't change your long-haul asset allocation unless your situation has changed. Market declines don't count. Revisit your long-term goals and your investment-growth models at least once a year, but not more than once every six months. Since investment performance varies widely from year to year—a fact you knew when you first set up the spreadsheet—it will take several years for you to assess whether your 20-year plan is working.

At the end of every year, revisit your retirement-planning model and write the current value of the portfolio in a new column next to the estimated value. Using your actual portfolio value, let the model tell you whether the projections still call for you to meet your investment objectives. If, over a multiyear period, you identify a trend that puts your goals in jeopardy, then make a change to fix the problem. You might have to invest more money or target a higher return. If those changes won't work for you, change your tack and consider scaling back your long-term goals.

WHEN TO RECONSIDER YOUR PLANS

Regardless of how long it's been since you reviewed your asset allocation or how close you come to meeting your goals, always revisit your long-term goals after a life change. The following events tend to alter the way we look at our investments, and might call for a major modification of our portfolio structure:

1. **Marriage.** They say two people can live as cheaply as one. That may or may not be true, but you should still take another look at your financial goals, because they are no longer just your individual goals. Your spouse's input could change some of the priorities, while a second income may make some dreams you'd dismissed as outlandish look more possible.

2. **The birth of a child.** With new children comes new expenses. Your month-to-month costs will rise, but of more relevance to investment plans, you need to think about setting aside money for college. Yes, it seems early. But by now you've learned enough about the power of time to know that college expenses will be easier to cover after 18 years of investing than if you wait until the boy starts high school.

3. **A new job or promotion.** Every time your job description or paycheck changes, go back to your financial projections. Can you set more aside than you originally planned? Will the new position affect the timing or magnitude of any of the goals you recorded?

4. **Divorce.** Nobody likes to think that their marriage will some day come to an end. But sometimes it will, and divorce takes more than an emotional toll on a couple. Your financial condition will change after the divorce, possibly affecting your long-term financial goals.

5. **An illness, deteriorating health of a parent, desire to purchase a vacation home, early retirement, and so forth.** Any time you learn you'll need a large chunk of money at a future time, create a new financial model to deal with it. Of course, because you have a finite amount of money to invest, your new model may not work unless you adjust the other models to accommodate the investment cash needed.

In the short run, the market is a voting machine, but in the

long run, the market is a weighing machine.

BENJAMIN GRAHAM
AUTHOR OF *THE INTELLIGENT INVESTOR*

12

MINIMIZE YOUR TAXES

Nobody likes paying taxes. There's a reason that people have equated taxes with death since the early 1700s, reflecting both distaste about ponying up the money and the difficulty of avoiding the cost. However, investors cannot afford to take this concept too far. Sure, you can take steps to limit your tax burden. But once you start making investment decisions with tax avoidance as your chief concern, you can count on making foolish decisions.

Better to have profits with a hefty tax bill than no profits to tax. The prior statement is inarguably logical, yet many smart investors seem to forget it. Don't be among them. Don't invest to limit your taxes. Invest to maximize your returns, within a structure that limits taxes on those returns. Remember that tax laws change constantly, and today's tax-minimizing strategies may not work tomorrow.

Retirement Accounts

While you may not wish to put in the time to become a tax expert (few investors do), anyone can take advantage of some of the simpler and more powerful tax-avoidance tools the government makes available. The single best tax-minimizing move available to most investors involves government-sanctioned retirement accounts. Stash as much of your investment funds as possible in these accounts since they are not subject to taxes.

TAX RATES

The following tax rates applied as of July 2014 and could change at any time. While the massive U.S. tax code allows for plenty of exceptions and special cases, the bullets that follow should reflect most tax situations investors will face.

- **Ordinary income.** A sliding scale based on income tops out at a 39.6 percent income tax. High-income taxpayers may also face a 3.8 percent health care surtax.

- **Dividends.** You'll pay up to 20 percent in taxes on qualified dividends, which includes most dividends paid by U.S. corporations and corporations in foreign countries that have signed tax treaties with the United States. This tax rate varies based on income, with some taxpayers paying 15 percent and low-income Americans paying no tax on dividends. Nonqualified dividends (which include capital-gain distributions, dividends on bank deposits, payments from tax-exempt organizations, and a few other unusual situations) are taxed at an ordinary-income rate. To receive the lower tax rates on qualified dividends, you must satisfy a holding-period requirement, owning a stock for 60 days of the 121-day period that begins 60 days before the stock's ex-dividend date. The ex-dividend date is the first day after a company declares the dividend when the stock's buyer (as opposed to the seller) is entitled to the dividend. Most of the time, if you hold a stock for 90 days, you're fine.

- **Interest.** Interest payments made by most bonds are taxed at the ordinary income rate. The chief exception? Interest paid by municipal bonds is generally exempt from federal taxes.

- **Capital gains.** In most cases, profits from the sale of securities or property held for more than one year (long-term capital gains) are taxed at the same rate as qualified dividends. Gains on collectibles and some types of small-business stock and real property face higher rates. The IRS taxes short-term capital gains at the ordinary income rate.

401(k) Plans

These retirement plans allow employers to defer some of your salary, transferring it into investments without you being responsible for the taxes. In other words, if you earn $50,000 a year and put $5,000 into a 401(k) plan, you'll pay taxes only on the $45,000. In 2014, employees could contribute up to $17,500 to a 401(k), with those over age 50 allowed to make an additional $5,500 in catch-up contributions.

Funds in a 401(k) plan can grow tax-free, with investors paying taxes only when they withdraw the cash. You must start taking money out of the plan after you reach age 70½, or in some cases right after you retire.

Many employers contribute money to their employees' 401(k) plans, often tying the contributions to the amount the employees choose to set aside. Most employers hire professional money managers to handle their 401(k) plans and allow employees to choose where to direct their contributions. The quality of the investment options varies widely from plan to plan, so research the choices available.

While 401(k) plans are designed to fund an employee's retirement, you can take money out to cover certain hardships, though you may be assessed a 10 percent penalty for early withdrawal. Some plans allow the employee to take out a loan against the assets. Then there are traditional IRAs (individual retirement arrangements), like 401(k) plans, which allow investors to set aside money before paying taxes and grow the funds tax deferred. IRAs differ from 401(k) plans in several ways:

1. **Contribution limits.** In 2014, investors could contribute up to $5,500 to an IRA, with an extra $1,000 in catch-up contributions for those age 50 or older.
2. **Self-administration.** You must set up your own IRA, generally through a brokerage or bank, and manage it yourself. That self-management gives an investor freedom to select a wide range of investments rather than being limited by the offerings of an employer's 401(k) plan. However, that same freedom requires more responsibility, as you won't benefit from the forced-saving approach of the 401(k).
3. **Deductibility.** If you or your spouse already participates in a retirement plan at work, you may not be able to deduct IRA contributions.

Roth IRAs and 401(k) Plans

Roth IRAs are derivations of the traditional IRA and 401(k) that allow investors to grow their assets tax free rather than tax deferred. Contributions to the Roth plans are not tax deductible, in that you make them using after-tax dollars. However, any withdrawals at retirement are made with no tax liability.

The Roth versions of the IRA and 401(k) differ from their traditional brethren in other ways as well, most notably limitations on contributions to Roth IRAs for investors who exceed certain income thresholds.

Before you decide which type of retirement plan to use, do some research and select the one that makes the most sense for you. There are no hard-and-fast rules regarding which type of investments you should put in tax-deferred plans versus which types you should leave in taxable plans or whether a Roth or traditional IRA makes more sense for you. Many of these decisions fall back to personal preference. Regardless of your preferences for one type of account over another, follow these three rules to minimize your tax hit:

1. **Take advantage of tax protections.** Only stash money in a taxable account after you've reached your contribution limits for tax-deferred or tax-free plans.

SEVEN TAX-REDUCTION TIPS

1. **Offset losses.** Just as you can earn capital gains when you sell stocks, bonds, or real estate at a profit, you can generate capital losses when you sell at a loss. Individuals can deduct up to $3,000 in losses against other taxable income each year. If you have losses in taxable accounts, don't forget to use them to reduce your tax liability. Losses of more than $3,000 can be saved for use in future years.

2. **Max out your 401(k).** For most people, the 401(k) offers the greatest chance to build wealth tax-deferred. Unless your plan's investment options are weak, contribute as much as you can to your 401(k). At the very least, set aside enough to max out your employer's matching contributions. That's as close as most people will ever come to earning free money.

3. **Hold your stocks for a year.** If a stock or bond becomes toxic and timing matters, sell it regardless of how long you've held it. But if you're deciding whether to sell a security that you've owned for nearly a year and feel no rush to get out, consider keeping it long enough for it to qualify as a long-term capital gain. Long-term capital gains enjoy lower tax rates than short-term gains.

4. **Don't overdo it.** Tax avoidance reflects good financial management. Tax evasion is illegal and can send you to prison. Know the line between the two and never cross it.

5. **Remember your costs.** If you spent $20 in commissions to buy a $1,000 position in a stock, that stock's cost basis (the original value of an asset for tax purposes) is $1,020—the amount of the investment plus the commission. For frequent traders, commission costs can add up.

6. **Keep good records.** A common mistake made by investors involves a failure to take into account reinvested dividends. Suppose you invest $10,000 in a mutual fund and reinvest the $300 a year it pays in dividends into the fund. Along the way, you'll pay taxes on those dividends. Five years later, you sell the fund for $20,000. Because you put $1,500 in dividends back into the fund, your capital gain would be $8,500 ($20,000 − $10,000 − $1,500), not the $10,000 implied by the purchase and sale price. Pay close attention to any tax information you receive that is connected to your investments. If you don't understand it, seek help.

7. **Consult a professional.** If you know about taxes, then prepare your own returns if you like. But the tax code is dense and complicated. Investors who are unsure of how to classify their income should consider paying someone else to do their taxes.

2. **Be consistent.** Government limits on the amount you can contribute to 401(k) plans and IRAs cap the size of your retirement portfolio. Suppose you set aside nothing this year and $35,000 next year instead of $17,500 this year and the same next year. Twenty years from now, your total portfolio may barely notice the difference, depending on the market return for those first two years. But if your lopsided investments forced half of that money to go into taxable accounts, you could end up paying a lot more in taxes over the long run.

3. **Pay attention.** Don't be the last one to know when tax laws change. Follow the news and adjust your tax strategies accordingly.

Resources

STOCK AND FINANCIAL-MARKET ANALYSIS

- Finance.yahoo.com
- Money.msn.com
- Google.com/finance

BOND ANALYSIS

- Bondsonline.com
- You can also find some bond-related information free of charge at the Yahoo!, MSN, and Google sites listed above.

FUND ANALYSIS

- Morningstar.com provides data on more than 160,000 mutual funds and nearly 11,000 ETFs, including multiple share classes for many funds.

RESEARCHING PROPERTY

- *U.S. Census Bureau*: (Census.gov) provides demographic and population information
- *Google*: (Google.com) provides searches by zip code
- *City-Data*: (City-data.com) provides demographic information
- *U.S. Chamber of Commerce*: (USchamber.com) provides information about businesses operating in a given city or state
- *U.S. Bureau of Labor Statistics*: (BLS.gov) provides information about employment trends
- *LoopNet*: (LoopNet.com) The Market Trends feature provides information on the space available for rent in an area as well as the actual rents and the amounts others are trying to collect.
- *LoopNet, CoStar, and Realtor.com*: (CoStar.com, Realtor.com) provide property listings

SMALL BUSINESS RESOURCES

- Small Business Administration (SBA.gov)
- SCORE (SCORE.org)
- International Franchise Association (Franchise.org)

FURTHER READING

Bernstein, William J. *The Intelligent Asset Allocator: How to Build Your Portfolio to Maximize Returns and Minimize Risk*. New York: McGraw Hill, 2001.

Lesonsky, Lieva, and Entrepreneur Media. *Start Your Own Business: The Only Startup Book You'll Ever Need*. Irvine, CA: Entrepreneur Press, 2007.

Libava, Joel. *Become a Franchise Owner! The Start-Up Guide to Lowering Risk, Making Money, and Owning What You Do*. Hoboken, NJ: Wiley, 2012.

Martinka, John. *Buying a Business That Makes You Rich: Toss Your Job Not the Dice*. Bothell, WA: Book Publishers Network, 2013.

Tycho Press. *Personal Finance Simplified*. Berkeley, CA: Tycho, 2014.

Tycho Press. *Stock Market Investing for Beginners: Essentials to Start Investing Successfully*. Berkeley, CA: Tycho, 2014.

Tycho Press. *Real Estate Investing for Beginners*. Berkeley, CA: Tycho, 2014.

References

Bankrate. "Mortgage Calculator." Accessed July 11, 2014. www.bankrate.com
/calculators/mortgages/mortgage-calculator.aspx.

BarclayHedge. "Assets under Management." Accessed June 2, 2014.
www.barclayhedge.com/research/money_under_management.html.

Berardino, Mike. "Mike Tyson Explains One of His Most Famous Quotes."
Sun Sentinel, November 9, 2012. http://articles.sun-sentinel.com/2012-11-09
/sports/sfl-mike-tyson-explains-one-of-his-most-famous-quotes-20121109_1
_mike-tyson-undisputed-truth-famous-quotes.

Christenson, Gary. "Silver Price in the Last 100 Years." *GoldSilverWorlds*, February
18, 2014. http://goldsilverworlds.com/price/silver-price-in-the-last-100-years/.

CNNMoney. "How Much Will That College Really Cost?" Accessed May 26, 2014.
http://cgi.money.cnn.com/tools/collegecost/collegecost.html.

CNNMoney. "Will You Have Enough to Retire?" Accessed May 26, 2014.
http://money.cnn.com/calculator/retirement/retirement-need/.

College Savings Plans Network. "College Cost Calculator." Accessed May 26, 2014.
www.collegesavings.org/collegeCostCalculator.aspx.

Dahl, Darren. "Top 10 Reasons to Run Your Own Business." *Inc.* Last updated
January 21, 2011. www.inc.com/guides/201101/top-10-reasons-to-run-your
-own-business.html.

Ennico, Cliff. "Before You Buy That Small Business." *Entrepreneur*. June 18, 2008.
www.entrepreneur.com/article/195020.

Internal Revenue Service. "Dividends and Other Distributions." Accessed
June 14, 2014. www.irs.gov/publications/p17/ch08.html.

Internal Revenue Service. "Do You Need an EIN?" Accessed June 7, 2014. www.irs.gov
/Businesses/Small-Businesses-&-Self-Employed/Do-You-Need-an-EIN.

Internal Revenue Service. "Individual Retirement Arrangements (IRAs)."
Accessed June 14, 2014. www.irs.gov/Retirement-Plans/Individual-Retirement
-Arrangements-(IRAs)-1.

Internal Revenue Service. "Retirement Topics—401(k) and Profit-Sharing Plan Contribution Limits." Last updated July 3, 2014. www.irs.gov/Retirement-Plans /Plan-Participant,-Employee/Retirement-Topics--401k-and-Profit-Sharing -Plan-Contribution-Limits.

Internal Revenue Service. "Topic 409—Capital Gains and Losses." Last updated February 27, 2014. www.irs.gov/taxtopics/tc409.html.

International Franchise Association. "What Are the Advantages and Disadvantages of Owning a Franchise?" Accessed June 7, 2014. www.franchise.org /franchiseesecondary.aspx?id=52630.

InvestinginBonds.com. "Bond Basics." Accessed May 30, 2014. www.investinginbonds.com/learnmore.asp?catid=46&id=5.

Investment Company Institute. "2013 Investment Company Fact Book." Accessed May 26, 2014. www.icifactbook.org.

Investment Company Institute. "Frequently Asked Questions about 401(k) Plans." Last updated February 2013. www.ici.org/policy/retirement/plan/401k /faqs_401k.

Investment Company Institute. "Trends in Mutual Fund Investing, May 2014." Accessed July 28, 2014. www.ici.org/research/stats/trends/trends_05_14.

Investopedia. http://investopedia.com.

Investopedia Staff. "10 Tips for Choosing an Online Broker." Investopedia. February 26, 2009. www.investopedia.com/articles/00/112100.asp.

Merriam-Webster. www.merriam-webster.com.

Morningstar. "Morningstar, Inc. Fact Sheet." May 2014. http://corporate.morningstar.com/US/documents/MarketingFactSheets /AboutMorningstarFactsheet.pdf.

National Council of Real Estate Investment Fiduciaries. "NCREIF Property Index Returns." Accessed June 7, 2014. www.ncreif.org/property-index-returns.aspx.

Rieman, Maxime. "Study: Only 24% of Active Mutual Fund Managers Outperform the Market Index." NerdWallet. March 27, 2013. www.nerdwallet.com/blog/ investing/2013/active-mutual-fund-managers-beat-market-index/.

Santoli, Michael. "The Stock Market Is 'Shrinking,' Despite Record-High Indexes." Yahoo! Returns. December 6, 2013. http://finance.yahoo.com/blogs/michael -santoli/the-stock-market-is-shrinking-despite-record-high-indexes -171141756.html.

SBA.gov. "10 Steps to Starting a Business." Accessed June 7, 2014. www.sba.gov /content/follow-these-steps-starting-business.

Securities and Exchange Commission, Office of Investor Education and Advocacy. "Investor Bulletin: Accredited Investors." Accessed June 2, 2014. www.sec.gov /investor/alerts/ib_accreditedinvestors.pdf.

Shapiro, Fred. "Quotes Uncovered: Death and Taxes." *Freakonomics.* February 17, 2011. http://freakonomics.com/2011/02/17/quotes-uncovered-death-and-taxes/.

Shrout, Kurt. "The U.S. Bond Market May Be Much Different Than You Think It Is." http://LearnBonds.com. May 30, 2013. www.learnbonds.com/how-big-is-the -bond-market/.

Terzo, Geri. "Typical Stockbroker Fees." Zacks. Accessed May 30, 2014. http://finance.zacks.com/typical-stockbroker-fees-7119.html.

ThreeTypes.com. "Part II: The 3 Types of Income." Accessed May 28, 2014. www.threetypes.com/philosophy/the-3-types-of-income/.

U.S. Census Bureau. "Statistics about Business Size (including Small Business) from the US Census Bureau: Employers and Nonemployers." Accessed June 7, 2014. www.census.gov/econ/smallbus.html.

Vanguard. "Transcript: Don't Overlook Your Asset Allocation as Life Changes." Accessed June 8, 2014. http://retirementplans.vanguard.com/VGApp/pe /pubnews/OverlookAssetAlocTranscript.jsf.

"Warren Buffett: His Best Quotes." *Telegraph*, February 14, 2013. www.telegraph.co .uk/finance/newsbysector/banksandfinance/8381363/Warren-Buffett-his-best -quotes.html.

Webb, Anthony, and Natalia A. Zhivan. "What Is the Distribution of Lifetime Health Care Costs from Age 65?" Center for Retirement Research at Boston College. February 2010. http://crr.bc.edu/wp-content/uploads/2010/02/IB_10-4.pdf.

Glossary

401(k) plan: An employer-sponsored retirement plan that allows workers to grow their retirement savings tax-free. Employers often provide matching contributions.

Bond: Debt issued by a corporation or government entity that agrees to repay the funds at a set time and also pay a defined rate of interest to compensate the lender.

Budget: An estimate of income and costs over a particular time period.

Capital gain: The increase in value of an asset, such as real estate or a financial security like a stock or a bond. Investors usually face a tax liability on the increase in value relative to the asset's purchase prices, but in most cases they need not pay taxes on such gains until they sell the asset. When property declines in value below its purchase price, an investor incurs a capital loss.

Cash flow: A stream of revenue. In a real estate context, most cash flows come from rents and leases. If expenses exceed revenue, cash flows will turn negative, possibly forcing the property owner to chip in her own funds to cover costs.

Deduction: A cost subtracted from taxable income. Expenses that qualify as deductible allow an investor to reduce tax liability.

Diversification: The use of multiple investments to protect against weakness in some portions of the market. Investors who own a diverse basket of investments can theoretically earn higher returns with lower risk than most of the investments would on their own. Real estate is a powerful diversification tool relative to more widely held investments, such as stocks and bonds.

Dividend: A portion of a company's earnings distributed to shareholders.

Exchange-traded fund (ETF): An investment vehicle made up of a pool of funds collected from many investors—similar to a mutual fund, but traded on an exchange like a stock. The funds are used to invest in securities such as stocks or bonds.

Franchise: A license awarded by a company (the franchisor) to a party (the franchisee) that provides the franchisee access to a company's brand and business processes. Most of the time, in effect a franchise allows an investor to operate a business with a large company's name on the marquee.

Hedge: An investment designed to reduce the risk of poor returns for a particular asset. For example, an investor who owns a stock index might protect herself against declines in that index by purchasing a futures contract that rises in value when the index falls. Because real estate tends to increase in value during periods of high inflation, it serves as a partial hedge against declines in other investments that react poorly to rising consumer prices.

Individual retirement arrangement (IRA): A tax-deferred investment account.

Interest: The charge for the privilege of borrowing money, typically expressed as an annual percentage rate. Borrowers who take out loans pay interest to the lender. Savings deposits pay interest to depositors as compensation for the bank being allowed to hold and use the funds.

Leverage: The use of borrowed money to finance the purchase of property. Debt allows investors to acquire real estate worth far more than their cash on hand. However, payments on that debt raise the risk that the property's cash flows won't cover all the expenses. An investor who has borrowed a lot of money relative to the value of the property is said to be highly leveraged.

Loan: A sum of money borrowed, generally expected to be repaid with interest.

Loan-to-value ratio: The amount borrowed relative to the worth of the property. If a bank allows an investor to borrow at a loan-to-value ratio of 75%, he can acquire a $1 million office building by putting up $250,000 in cash (25% of the value) while the bank provides the remaining $750,000 (75% of the value).

Management fee: A charge paid by mutual-fund investors to compensate the people who make investment decisions for the fund, generally reflected as a percentage of the assets.

Mortgage: A loan secured by real estate. Borrowers must pay the loan back in regularly scheduled installments, generally over a number of years. Because of the long terms of mortgage loans, in the early years, most of a borrower's payments will go toward interest, with little paying down the loan's principal.

Mutual fund: An investment vehicle made up of a pool of funds collected from many investors. The funds are used to invest in securities such as stocks or bonds.

Portfolio: A group of financial assets such as stocks, bonds, and mutual funds.

Property manager: A person or company overseeing the day-to-day operations of a piece of real estate.

Real estate: Land and permanent structures erected on it.

Real estate investment trust (REIT): A company that invests directly in real estate and sells ownership interests through exchanges like a stock. REITs can own either real property or mortgage loans. These companies enjoy special tax treatment that allows them to return higher cash flows to investors than most stocks can offer. Through REITs, investors can purchase a stake in the real estate market without the liquidity risk (you can sell REITs in real time just like stocks) or the hassles of managing property.

Return: The gain or loss of an investment in a given period. Returns include both income and capital gains, or price appreciation.

Risk-adjusted return: A measurement of an investment's return relative to the amount of risk needed to produce that return.

Risk tolerance: How much volatility an investor can take. Willingness and ability to absorb investment fluctuations varies greatly from person to person. Investors of any tolerance can make money, but they can improve their odds by not taking on more risk than they can handle. Too much risk can spark fear, which in turn leads to poor investment decisions.

Sales load: A fee charged to purchasers of mutual funds as compensation to the individual or company that sells the fund. This fee is above and beyond the management fee.

Standard deviation: A measurement of how widely returns are dispersed around the average. The broader the variation, the higher the standard deviation, and thus the greater an investment's volatility, or risk.

Stock: An ownership interest in a company. Over long periods, stocks tend to provide higher returns than bonds or real estate, but at the cost of greater volatility.

Thrill seeker: An investor who craves risk, often more than is wise, in an effort to glean excitement from the investing process.

Worrier: An investor who focuses on the downside more than the upside, often taking on less risk than is wise, and as such generating weaker returns.

Yield: The ratio of dividends or other cash payouts to the price of a security. For example, if a REIT trades at $50 per share and pays an annual dividend of $2.50 per share, it yields 5% (2.50/50).

Source: Investopedia.

Index

CPSIA information can be obtained at www.ICGtesting.com
Printed in the USA
LVOW07s1433210215

427768LV00001B/4/P